Living from the Center

Living from the Center

Spirituality in an Age of Consumerism

Jay McDaniel

Chalice Press®

St. Louis, Missouri

Cover photo: Gregory J. Lawler, Small Planet Photography
Cover design: Bob Currie
Interior design: Wynn Younker
Art direction: Michael Domínguez

This book is printed on acid-free, recycled paper.

Visit Chalice Press on the World Wide Web at
www.chalicepress.com

10 9 8 7 6 5 4 3 2   03 04 05

Library of Congress Cataloging–in–Publication Data

McDaniel, Jay B. (Jay Byrd), 1949–
    Living from the center : spirituality in an age of consumerism / by Jay McDaniel.
        p.   cm.
    ISBN 0-8272-2130-4
    1. Spirituality I. Title.
BV4501.2   .M2294   2000
248.4–dc21
                                                    00–010338

Printed in the United States of America

Contents

Acknowledgments

I wish to acknowledge the following authors and publishers for materials that have appeared in this book:

Booth, Philip. *First Lesson* from *Letters from a Distant Land.* Viking Penguin Inc. 1957.

Ferlinghetti, Lawrence. *Christ Climbed Down* from *A Coney Island of the Mind.* New York: New Directions.1958.

Oliver, Mary. *The Summer Day* from *A House of Light.* Boston: Beacon Press.

Rogers, Pattiann. *Distance and Depth* and *The Greatest Grandeur* from *Fire Keeper: New and Selected Poems.* Minneapolis: Milkweed Editions.

Scheele, Roy. *The Gap in the Cedar* from *Accompanied.* Best Cellar Press. 1974.

Stern, Gerald. *Lucky Life* from *Lucky Life.* New York: Houghton Mifflin Company.

Prologue

Consider the lilies of the field, how they grow; they neither toil nor spin, yet I tell you, even Solomon in all his glory was not clothed like one of these.

Matthew 6:28

Consider the lilies is the only commandment I ever obeyed.

Emily Dickinson[1]

I know a man who gets up in the morning, looks in the mirror, and finds himself asking, "Am I rich enough? Am I attractive enough? Am I successful enough? Am I famous yet?" He doesn't know that God loves him just as he is.

As the day unfolds, he then falls into a compulsive busyness, frenetically on his way toward a happiness that never quite arrives. He wants to be just a little more "successful" or "recognized" or "appreciated" than he is. He doesn't feel that he has "made it" yet. He wants his day in the sun.

I know his children too. They think that he is successful when he takes time to listen to them, when he plays basketball with them, when he helps them with their homework. They wish he would work less and relax more. They think that he has already "made it." They think that he is having his day in the sun when he is enjoying their companionship.

I know this man well, because sometimes I see him in the mirror. I am a typical, middle-class American who is too often distracted by the performance-based atmosphere of consumer culture, at the expense of becoming his better self. I write this book, not as an expert on spirituality in the age of consumerism, but as one who would like to live more spiritually than I presently do.

Of course, this is not the whole story. Even as people like me are influenced by consumerism, we also harbor a deeper dream that is not reducible to "making money" and "becoming a success." Inwardly, we want to live from wisdom, compassion, and freedom, not appearance, affluence, and achievement. We want to live from the Center.

1

Indeed, amid and despite the influences of consumerism, most of us already do live from the Center in certain moments of our lives. A friend needs help, a dog needs petting, a child needs a hug, a rose needs smelling—and we rise to the occasion. In the moment at hand, we transcend consumerism and live from a deeper image: not the image of a successful person we carry in our heads, but rather the image of God that resides in our hearts. In these moments we participate in God's Breathing and become more fully human.

Moreover, if we are lucky, we have role models who live from the Center even more consistently than we do. I think of my own father, who was a kind and gentle man. I think also of my wife, and a secretary I know, and a janitor, and a teacher, and a poet. Usually these people do not know that they are living from the Center, and their humility makes them all the more beautiful. Often they are not very interested in theology, and sometimes they are not very religious. As a theologian myself, I find this indifference to theology still more attractive.

In any case, these people live simply and wisely, frugally and compassionately, without need for acclaim or recognition, and with a grace sufficient to each moment. They are the people to whom you and I will turn when we need someone to talk to. These are saints in the age of consumerism. They are beyond appearance, affluence, and marketable achievement. They are hidden in Christ.

By Christ I do not mean Jesus. Rather, I mean what we might call the *Spirit of Christ.* I mean the indwelling spirit of God, which has been immanent within creation from the beginning, which was enfleshed but not exhausted in Jesus, and which can nourish our inner lives and outer actions still today. To be hidden in Christ is to be hidden from the world of consumer-driven acclaim, to be hidden in the deeper reality of God's Breathing, and, by virtue of this hiddenness, to be authentically responsive to the situation at hand. It is to live from the Center.

In our world many people are hidden in Christ. Some are female and some are male. Some are employed and some are unemployed. Some have families and some are alone. Some are funny and some are serious. Some are Japanese, some are Iranian, some are Nigerian, and some are Russian. Some are Buddhist, some are Jewish, some are Muslim, some are Hindu. Some belong to no religion whatsoever. In their simplicity and gentleness, in their freedom from busyness, they are like flowers in a forest, blossoming forth in beauty, without needing to be recognized, and all the more beautiful for their hiddenness. We have much to learn from them.

But even if we lack such models of post-consumer hiddenness, even if we feel all alone in our desire to live spiritually in the age of consumerism, we are not devoid of spiritual teachers. Other creatures, too, can be hidden in Christ.

Consider the lilies of the field. The real ones. Jesus indicates that we have as much to learn from them as from the angels in heaven. He is not arguing against angels. Our universe may well contain multiple planes of existence, some of which are inhabited by healing spirits. Others may even be inhabited by less kindly beings. If an angel comes to visit you, I suggest that you listen. I will do the same. Let's watch out for the demons too.

But the lilies also have something important to say, not in words but in sheer presence. In their naturalness and spontaneity, in their receptivity to the breath of life, they embody the heart of spirituality. They find God in the present moment.

I think this is what Emily Dickinson had in mind when she remarked that the only commandment she ever obeyed was to consider the lilies. She rightly reminds us that our deepest calling in life—the greatest of Jesus' commandments—is not to make money or become famous or have a successful career. Rather, it is to be open to God in a distinctively human way, as are lilies in their distinctively herbal way. It is to consider and then imitate the lilies.

My subject, then, is lily imitation—spirituality—in the age of consumerism. By spirituality I mean *openness to God's Breathing, day by day and moment by moment, relative to the circumstances at hand.* Understood in this way, spirituality is not supernatural or extraordinary, but deeply natural and wholly ordinary. It can be embodied at home and in the workplace, while alone and with others, amid dish washing and diaper changing, laughing and crying, living and dying. Indeed, spirituality can even be present in boredom if we are patient with our boredom and do not think that we must be excited all the time. Spirituality is ordinary life itself, as obedient to the call of the moment, as lived from a deeper Center.

This deeper Center has many names. Some people call it the *Breath of Life;* others call it the *Spirit of God;* others call it the *Holy Spirit;* and still others call it the *Indwelling Presence of God* or the *Tao.* In this book I usually call it the *Freshness Deep Down* and *God's Breathing.* Above I also called it the *Spirit of Christ.* However we name it, it is always more than our names. It belongs to a world beyond creeds and doctrines, a world beyond words, a world beyond religion. It is a healing and creative spirit by which the universe itself has been called into existence, moment by moment, over its fifteen-billion-year history, which resides within each living being as a lure toward the fullness of life relative to the situation at hand, and which resides within each human being as a lure toward wisdom, compassion, and freedom. It is the Center of the universe and the center of our lives.

Of course, this Breathing is not a Center in any ordinary sense. It is not located in a particular region of space. Rather, it is everywhere at once: equally present to the most distant of galaxies, the smallest of microbes, the most ordinary of sparrows, the most vulnerable of children, and the most heinous of criminals. To be sure, people are not always present to the Spirit. Witness the rape and murder, the callousness and confusion, the envy and greed in the world. But the Spirit is always present to them, to us. There is nowhere we can go, not even to hell, where the Spirit is not already present.

Accordingly, each living being on our planet has its own way of being open to this Spirit, its own way of praying. Here prayer does not mean talking to God or even believing in God. It means being available to the Spirit, relative to what is possible for the creature at issue. For many creatures, this availability comes naturally and instinctively, without special intention. Birds pray by flying, fish by swimming, cats by purring, dogs by barking, and lilies by flowering. Just in being themselves, they pray.

How, then, do we pray? What is our human analogue to the swimming of fish, the purring of cats, the barking of dogs, and the flowering of lilies? We pray by becoming wise, compassionate, and free in our daily lives, day by day and moment by moment. Whenever these three qualities emerge in our lives—consciously or unconsciously, intentionally or unintentionally—we are listening and responding to God. We are joining the larger dance of creation. We are praying.

Thus, we have another way of defining spirituality. It is not only openness to the Spirit of God relative to the situation at hand; it is also what happens when, even if only for a moment, we enter into wisdom, compassion, and freedom: into prayerful living. When we enter into this living, prayer is not really something we do; rather, it is something we are. I hope that in some small way this book helps you and me alike to become prayer.

Of course, there are many good books on prayer and spirituality. Perhaps too many. When we walk into bookstores and see the abundance of them, we sometimes find ourselves believing that we must read just one more book on prayer before we can pray ourselves. We forget that the Spirit was breathing in the universe long before books were invented. We forget that even the animals can pray. Even the stars.

Still, I encourage you to read one more book. If there is justification for my request, perhaps it is that I will be using three sources that are not often combined and that, in combination, can add fresh insights to familiar themes. They are process theology, Buddhism, and contemplative Christianity.

In the Introduction I will explain these sources and tell you how I arrived at the decision to use them. You will discover that I am a recovering Christian fundamentalist who struggles every day of my life with the realities of consumerism and who is trying to become a better Christian with the help of Buddhism. For now, however, I want to offer some observations about this book's style. In writing this book, six ideals have guided me.

Six Ideals

First, I have wanted to write in a way that is accessible to the general reader and not just the academic. I am trained in the philosophy of religion and theology, and I have written to audiences similarly trained. But over the years I have grown impatient with the tendency of academic theologians such as I to talk primarily to members of their guild. I fear that we have lost touch, not only with our readers, but also with some of the deeper promptings of the human heart.

Second, I have wanted to combine images with concepts, trustful that truth is found in both, neither to the exclusion of the other. Thus, in the pages that follow, you will find as many stories from personal experience and parables borrowed from poems as you will more abstract concepts. Here, too, this represents a change in my own perspective. There was once a time when I thought there was more truth in concepts than images, in philosophy than poetry. I was an English literature major in college who minored in philosophy, but I always thought I should have majored in philosophy and minored in English. I thought Aristotle possessed more truth than Emily Dickinson. But things have changed. I have come to believe that some of the most important insights we can gain concerning God and life come through images and stories and the feelings evoked by them. Emily Dickinson seems as wise as, if not sometimes wiser than, Aristotle.

Third, I have wanted to speak to people of other religions and no religion, trustful that the Spirit is not reducible to Christianity. For my part, I write as a Christian. God's way to me is through the healing presence of Jesus, to whom I try to entrust my heart, sometimes successfully and sometimes not. Indebted to the tradition that bears his name but that is so often unfaithful to him, I find myself interpreting many traditional Christian themes: God, Christ, Holy Spirit, church, death and resurrection, sacramentality, contemplation, discernment, the Second Coming, hiddenness in Christ, and eternal life. These themes come naturally to me. They are my language. If you are Christian, I hope you might find that some of my interpretations offer a fresh perspective on traditional themes.

Nevertheless, I also hope that these themes can speak to people of many different perspectives, not just to Christians. Even as I try to follow the way of Jesus, I do not think a person needs to believe in Jesus in order to follow him. I have met many people who are more faithful to Jesus than I, but who do not believe in him. I do not limit Christ to Christianity. If you belong to another religious tradition, I hope that you might translate what I have to say into your own terms. If you are Buddhist, for example, you might translate my words *God's Breathing* into *the Buddha-nature*, and you might translate *church* into your word for community, namely *Sangha*. If you are Jewish, you might translate my words *God's Breathing* into *Shekhinah*, or the indwelling presence of God, and you might translate *church* into *the house of Israel*. In each instance, though, you will need to stretch meanings beyond the familiar usage. You will need to recognize that even lilies of the field can be hidden in the Buddha-nature and members of the Sangha. You will need to say that even the Gentiles, in being obedient to God's call in the moment, can receive the indwelling presence of God and be unofficial members of the house of Israel. Of course, there are selected lineages within your own traditions that move in just this direction, just as there are lineages within Christianity that do the same.

Fourth, while spirituality can be a property of communities rather than individuals, I have tried to speak to the individual rather than the community. By *community* I mean a household, a neighborhood, a church or sangha, a group of friends in the workplace, a city, or a region. I also mean a group of people, a professional organization for example, who share a common interest and who are in communication with one another through periodic face-to-face meetings or with the help of e-mail and the Internet.

All these communities can participate in spirituality. All can be carriers of divine Breathing. Nevertheless, I focus on individuals rather than communities in this book, primarily because I think there is a private and personal dimension to spirituality that is neglected when we turn too quickly to discussions of community, and also because I want to speak to people who belong to many different kinds of communities, some healthy and some unhealthy. For example, I imagine that some of my readers live in relatively happy households, while others live in households fraught with tension. We dwell in different communities. Still, I think that, as individuals, we share common opportunities for being available to God's Breathing, relative to our different situations. I focus on individuals because I want to highlight our common opportunities.

Fifth, I have wanted to write a book that is anti-consumerism but pro-business. This may be an impossible task, and you can best be the judge. But I hope that a world can emerge in which the culture of business is liberated from the culture of consumerism, so that business, in balance with government and civic organizations, can itself be in greater service to community. Thus, as you read my numerous critiques of consumer culture, please understand that I am not opposed to the free enterprise system or to the creativity that that system unleashes, but rather to the values and attitudes that too often underlie that system when it is enslaved to consumerism. The great hope of the future, it seems to me, is that people who enter business can help transform business itself into a path of service, not greed. There are many businesspeople in the world who are already deeply spiritual and who desire this transformation. I hope this book offers a little help.

Sixth, in writing this book I have wanted to give an overview of the spiritual life, rather than focusing on one aspect of spirituality to the exclusion of others. This means that I try to treat many different aspects of spiritual living, ranging from compassion and creativity to delight in beauty and contemplative prayer, showing how they might be part of a larger experiential whole, which I call *openness to God's Breathing*. I well recognize that each of these aspects of spirituality deserves a book in its own right. I hope that my treatment might inspire you to ponder these themes more deeply. I do not offer an exhaustive treatment of any given theme, but rather meditations on many themes, all of which fit together.

This book is itself a series of meditations. I attend a church in which, after giving a sermon, the minister says, "May the words of my mouth and the meditations of my heart be acceptable in your sight, O Lord." My aim is to offer a series of meditations from my heart that I hope are acceptable in the Lord's sight but that, either way, may elicit meditations in your own heart, depending on your interests and situation. I trust that you can learn as much by disagreeing with what I have to say as by agreeing with it.

The book consists of an introduction, six chapters, and a conclusion. If there is a single part of the book that is most important, it is perhaps the Table of Contents, which includes not only the names of each chapter but also the various topics treated in a given chapter. I have written the book as if it would be read front to back, but it can also be read in a freer way. If you want to follow the lure of your own interests, I suggest that you begin with the Table of Contents, peruse the topics treated in the chapters, and then turn to the chapter at issue.

In some instances it is also possible simply to read sections of various chapters, one from this chapter and one from another. For example, in chapter 1, I identify nine ways of being open to God's Breathing, one of which is discernment, and in chapter 2, I offer five guidelines for discernment. It is possible to read the section on nine ways in chapter 1 and the section on five guidelines in chapter 2. I myself sometimes read books in this way. I encourage you to do the same. Let the Table of Contents be your guide.

A final word is in order about documentation. You will note that this book contains very few references to specific sources. This is not because I arrived at my ideas all on my own. I am not sure there is a single idea in this book that is original to me. Still, it remains the case that I do not give you many footnotes or endnotes. There is not even a bibliography. My reason may or may not be justified, but I can at least be honest. Given my personal circumstances as a father of two children, husband of one wife, and full-time college teacher, I have had little, if any, time to spend in the library poring over other books on spirituality in an age of consumerism. I have had to allow my own struggles with consumerism, and my own hopes for a more spiritually satisfying life than consumerism encourages, to be my laboratory.

Thus, if I were to give specific references, some of them would have to be "taking this trip to the mall" and "hearing this advertisement on the radio" and "seeing this billboard for Jesus." These kinds of experiences have been central to my own reflections on spirituality in an age of consumerism. I have not had to go very far to learn about consumerism. I find it in my home, my head, my heart, my church, and my community.

Nevertheless, I can happily name some of the specific sources that have shaped this book in a positive way. Please let this list of spiritual friends and guides substitute for a bibliography.

I want to thank the staff at the Shalem Institute for Spiritual Formation in Washington, D.C., particularly Tilden Edwards, Jerry

May, and Rosemary Dougherty. From Tilden I learned that wisdom, compassion, and freedom are the heart of spiritual living; from Jerry I learned that the spiritual life is an ongoing process of death and resurrection; and from Rosemary I learned that this life involves openness to our own inner wisdom. My comments on inner freedom and delight in beauty are particularly indebted to Tilden, on living-by-dying to Jerry, and on discernment to Rosemary. Much of this book springs from things that each of these three people said in workshops as I was participating in the Shalem's program on spiritual direction.

In addition, I want to thank Marcus Borg for his helpful work on the historical Jesus and his specific recommendation that Jesus offers an alternative to life based on appearance, affluence, and achievement; Reverend Keido Fukushima for his friendship for twenty-five years and for his guidance in, and example of, Zen meditation and Zen living; Professor John B. Cobb, Jr., for his friendship and for his guidance in, and example of, Christian living and Christian thinking in an age of consumerism; Thomas Berry for his friendship, his humility, and his consistent reminder that the universe is our primary revelation and that books and texts come second; the staff at the Center for Respect of Life and Environment in Washington, D.C., especially Dr. Richard Clugston and Tom Rogers, from whom I have learned so much about the state of the world, our need for a sustainable future, and the necessity of realizing that the universe is a communion of subjects, not a collection of objects; various poets—Coleman Barks, Philip Booth, Emily Dickinson, Lawrence Ferlinghetti Naomi Shihab Nye, Mary Oliver, Pattianne Rogers, Roy Scheele, Gerald Stern—whose images have offered so many hints into spiritual living; my friends at St. Peter's Episcopal Church and First United Methodist Church, who consistently revive my trust in the very possibility of organized religion to be a context for spiritual development; my friend Patricia Masters, who gave me the idea of being hidden in Christ; my friend Ann Young, who, along with Patricia Masters, offered invaluable suggestions on content and style; my colleagues in the Raney Building at Hendrix College, who teach me that education rightly includes companionship, laughter, and honest searching, not just "having the right answers"; my student assistant and friend Jason Alexander, who assisted me in final preparation of this manuscript by helping me gather permission to use various poems; the Journey into Silence meditation group, with whom I have enjoyed "quiet sitting in Zen style" on Monday nights, whose "journeys into silence" have helped quiet my own mind; and my wife Kathy, and two sons Matthew and Jason, each of whom suffered through far too many hours of my writing this book, displaying some of the most beautiful forms of spirituality there are: patience, forgiveness, and affection.

Finally, I want to thank some more-than-human beings. I first encountered this custom in the work of Mary Daly, the radical feminist philosopher, who footnotes dogs and cats in her book *Gyn/Ecology.*[2] Her custom always seemed right to me, as most of us are indeed indebted to the natural world for so much of what we think and do, if not also to companion animals who befriend us. Why not thank our nonhuman kin in a public way? Why pretend that we are all alone in a purely human world? Thus, I want to thank my two dogs, Ashes and Cinnamon, for their ever-present reminder that spirituality is not reducible to human beings, and from whom I have learned that playing, and also barking, can be a form of prayer; the Guadalupe River in the hill country of Texas, for its gentle reminder that rivers, no less than animals and plants, can be channels of grace in human life; and the dark and starlit sky, into which I sometimes gaze, and which nightly reveals a dark and womb-like grace in which we are all included, no matter how small and insignificant.

To the people and the dogs and the rivers and the sky, I say thank you. The mistakes are all mine. But the grace shines through you, and I am grateful for what I have received.

Introduction

Practicing the Presence

People were bringing little children to him...Jesus said...
"It is to such as these that the kingdom of God
belongs"...then he took them up in his arms.

Mark 10:13–16

One day, as I was working on this book, my young son Matthew came into the room and asked me if I would look at something he was drawing. Inwardly, I heard myself say, *I'm too busy. I'll do it later. I am doing something very important. I am writing a book. Can you wait?*

Of course, I am not at all proud of this voice. Nevertheless, I have heard it far too often. It is the voice of compulsive busyness and distraction: a kind of armor I wear in order to feel that I have purpose in life.

The good news is that, on this occasion, I did not heed the call of busyness. Matthew was quite tired of my having more important things to do. And I was tired of it too. What is more important than a young son who needs attention?

Moreover, as Matthew stood before me, there was a poem on my desk called "Welcome," which spoke quite directly to my situation. The poem is written by Naomi Shihab Nye and describes an Arab custom of welcoming strangers into one's house and feeding them for several days before asking about their business. The idea is that welcoming the stranger is at least as important as, if not much more important than, matters of commerce. The purpose of life, the poem seems to say, is not necessarily to get things done, but rather to be

11

present to others in a kind and caring way, day by day and moment by moment. It is to welcome the stranger.

My need, then, was to welcome my son. I could have uttered the third stanza of Nye's poem, from which I borrow the notion of busyness as armor. I could have said,

> No, I was not busy when you came!
>> I was not preparing to be busy.
>> That's just the armor everyone put on
>> At the end of the century
>> To pretend they had a purpose
> In the world.[1]

But instead of quoting poetry, I did something better. I turned off the computer, left the room, walked with him into the living room, and admired his drawing. I took off my armor of busyness and listened to my son.

Practicing the Presence of God

To an objective eye, this moment of listening was unremarkable. The evening news did not carry headlines saying "Busy man spends time with son." But I suspect that, in my moment of listening, I entered into God's purposes for my life at least as deeply as, and perhaps much more deeply than, in many other things I do. I begin this book with the proposal that the purpose of living is not to be hurried and frantic. It is to be fully present to where we are in ways that are wise, compassionate, and free.

How shall we name this attentive way of living? In this book I have various names for it: living from the Center, being available to God's Breathing, spirituality in the age of consumerism. But for now I borrow a phrase from a seventeenth-century Christian mystic traditionally called Brother Lawrence. He calls it "practicing the presence of God."[2]

This phrase is helpful in two ways. First, it suggests to us that, if God is to be present in our lives, we need to cooperate with that presence, intentionally or unintentionally, willingly or spontaneously. God cannot do it all alone; God needs us to be fully present in the world.

Second, the phrase suggests that God's presence and the world's presence are not entirely separate. We meet God in our lives—we practice the presence—by being open to others in gentle and loving ways. In their presence to us, God is present. In Matthew's presence to me, for example, God was present.

Part of my aim in this book, then, is to encourage you and me alike to practice the presence of God. It is to encourage us to become less distracted and more open, less frenetic and more faithful to our calling in each moment. In so doing, we can better appreciate the sacrament of each present moment.

For my part, I fall short of this calling far too often. I am a long way from being faithful to the calling of each present moment. Perhaps you are in a similar situation. Our respective reasons for being unfaithful may differ. The things that distract you from "welcoming the stranger" may be more legitimate. Nevertheless, I suspect that we have one problem in common. I suspect that we find ourselves compulsively busy because we are jointly influenced by a cultural atmosphere that emphasizes speed and busyness, productivity and progress, at the expense of being obedient to God's calling in each present moment. This cultural atmosphere could be named in many ways. We could call it hurriedness or freneticism or compulsivism. I call it consumerism. My subject, then, is spirituality in this age of consumerism.

The Problem of Consumerism

By consumerism I mean two things at once: (1) an overconsuming lifestyle, which is practiced by about one-fifth of the world's population and which leads to much environmental degradation and community disintegration; and (2) a set of attitudes and values, preached twenty-four hours a day, that reinforce this lifestyle.

My proposal in this book is that that these attitudes and values now function as an unofficial, corporate-sponsored world religion. Its evangelism occurs through advertisements, and its church is the mall. The window displays are its holy icons, and the credit card is its membership card. It tells us that we are saved or made whole—not by grace through faith as Christians claim, or by freedom through enlightenment as Buddhists claim—but by appearance, affluence, and marketable achievement.

Unfortunately, in our time, this religion influences every human being on the planet. People all over the world can recognize the logo of Nike shoes, even as they—we—forget the names of our neighbors. Certainly I am in this situation. I can remember the lyrics to many an ad for Coca Cola, having heard them all my life. I can say "Coke Is It" and "It's the Real Thing," humming the tunes I have heard on television. I have heard them so many times that they will be with me when I die.

But I cannot quite remember the name of the man who lives two houses down. Yes, he and I sometimes wave as we go to work. An observer might think we know each other. But I do not know how he is doing, what he loves about life, how his marriage is going, or whether his children are happy. When his corporation moves him to another city in several months, it will be as if he had never been my neighbor.

Of course, consumerism is not all bad. This cultural atmosphere—this religion—inspires enormous amounts of excitement and adventure, entertainment and creativity. When we stroll through the mall, we are understandably amazed at the amount of creativity that has gone into the design and packaging of jewelry, computers, guns, clothes, cosmetics, video games, toys, business supplies, pornography, medicines, music, and candy. We might wish that more creativity had gone toward the medicines and less toward the guns. We might insist that there are other forms of creativity, such as the creativity it takes to be a good homemaker, artist, or scientist.

Still, we are amazed by the amount of ingenuity that has gone into the creation of these materials. When a society is organized around the principle of producing consumer goods, much human creativity is unleashed. Such is the nature of a consumer society. It is a society in service to the ever-increasing production and consumption of material goods—that is, to economic growth.

Nevertheless, precisely in its unqualified commitment to economic growth, the consumer lifestyle also takes its toll on the earth, on communities, on families, and on the human soul. The social and environmental costs of consumerism have now been documented in many works.

Consider, for example, Alan Durning's *How Much is Enough? Consumer Society and the Fate of the Earth.*[3] In a chapter called "The Dubious Rewards of Consumerism," he shows how the rapid pace of the consumer lifestyle and the neglect of community have led so many into lives of compulsive busyness, envy, and acquisitiveness, despite their better intentions. According to studies cited by Durning, we consumers are no more happy, and in some ways less happy, than were earlier generations who had much less.

Additionally, in a chapter called "The Environmental Costs of Consumption," Durning shows how the environmental destruction of our planet is the result, not only of overpopulation and questionable technologies but also, and perhaps even more seriously, the overconsuming lifestyle and attitudes of consumer society. According to Durning, the overconsumers of the world, approximately one-fifth of the world's population, consume approximately 40 percent of its fresh water, 60 percent of its fertilizers, 75 percent of its energy, 75 percent of its timber, 80 percent of its paper, 85 percent of its aluminum. Our aerosol cans, air conditioners, and factories release almost 90 percent of the chlorofluorocarbons that cause ozone depletion. Our use of fossil fuels causes two-thirds of the emissions of carbon dioxide. If the whole world consumed as we consumed and polluted as we pollute, the life-support systems of our planet would quickly collapse. In Durning's words, "From global warming to species extinction, we overconsumers bear a huge burden of responsibility for the ills of the earth."[4]

I write this book as a companion to books like *How Much is Enough?* not as a substitute for such books. My aim is to begin with Durning's conclusion:

> The future of life on earth depends on whether we among the richest fifth of the world's people, having fully met our material needs, can turn to nonmaterial sources of fulfillment. Whether we—who have defined the tangible goals of world development—can now craft a new way of living at once simpler and more satisfying.[5]

My question is straightforward: Is there *truly* a way that is simpler and more satisfying? Can we *really* live less acquisitively and more meaningfully, less selfishly and more happily, for our sake and for the world's sake?

I think we can. Accordingly, I write this book for people of different religions and also no religion, who sense that there is more to life than appearance, affluence, and marketable achievement and who wish instead to live from a deeper Center. I want to describe this better way so that we might embody it in our daily lives. It is the Great Work.

The Great Work

The Great Work, then, is not a salaried job or a career. Rather, it is a calling. It lies in being faithful to the call of the moment, at home or in the workplace, while alone or with others, amid sound and silence, and in responding to this call from the deep place, from the Freshness.

Fortunately, we do not have to become someone else in order to participate in the Great Work. We can participate in this calling as accountants, poets, homemakers, parents, teachers, nurses, nuns, grandmothers, or clowns. Our Great Work can involve being good parents to our children, good children to our parents, good listeners to our friends, good friends to our neighbors, good forgivers of our foes, good participants in our communities, good companions to animals, and good friends of the Earth. It can also involve being good lovers of solitude, good laughers, good cryers, good readers of poetry, good listeners to music, good walkers in the woods, and good relaxers on holy days. Indeed, it can involve being good contributors to a business enterprise, if that business is producing a good or service that is truly beneficial to the world. But whatever its character, the Great Work is by no means reducible to making money. It is active cooperation with God's Breathing relative to the needs of the world and the circumstances at hand.

There is much creativity in this work, much joy, much gladness. I think it is even more creative than the kind of creativity that produces guns and candy, pornography and soft drinks. But it is also quieter and deeper. The writer Frederick Buechner puts it well. He says that the place to which God calls us is the place where our deep gladness meets the world's deep hungers.[6] The Great Work is to go to this place, live from its freshness, and love our neighbors as ourselves.

For my part, I am not sure there is anything more important in life. Openness to God's Breathing—to the Freshness Deep Down—is what gives life its meaning. Consumer society encourages us all to be entrepreneurs. I think we are called to be cooperators with God's Breathing.

Spirituality

Not just cooperators, but inhalers. Spirituality is not simply a path that we enter but also a path that enters us. Or perhaps better, a path that wells up within us, much as living water wells up from an underground spring. To practice the presence of God is not simply to cooperate with God's will in our lives, as if God were entirely external. Rather, it is to awaken to that Breathing as it already exists within the depths of our existence and then to allow that Breathing to animate our inner lives, such that we are, as it were, breathed by the Breathing.

The spiritual ingredients of God's Breathing are wisdom, compassion, and interior freedom. When these three ingredients enter our lives—even for a moment—it is as if the darkened windows had been opened in a confining and suffocating room, and fresh air had entered our lungs. The fresh air is divine Breathing. The suffocating room is our heart as enclosed and contracted by the cramping confines of our ego. The darkened windows are the boundaries that have been placed between ourselves and the world, and between ourselves and divine Breathing. They are what make the room so confining.

Some of these darkened windows—these boundaries—are of our own making. They consist of the greeds, hatreds, and confusions into which we have fallen through decisions we have made in the past, which have then become habits of the heart. They become manifest as compulsive hurriedness, compulsive acquisitiveness, and compulsive envy. They shut us off from the world and our own better selves.

Other darkened windows have been given to us. They include selfish attitudes and feelings that we inherit from our culture and surroundings, and also diseases and destructive impulses that we inherit from our bodies. A young boy who is brought up in a family that is filled with hatred of people of other cultures will feel the feelings of his family and be influenced by those feelings. He will feel hatred too. It is not his fault that he was brought up by this family, but his windows have been darkened and shut nevertheless. Similarly, a young woman who is brought up in a consumer-driven home, in which she is taught by her parents that "being attractive" and "making money" are what life is all about, will inevitably inherit these values as part of her psychic makeup.

The good news is that these windows can be opened, regardless of how they might have been closed. Always this opening occurs with the help of the universe: friends and strangers, plants and animals, spirits and ancestors, rivers and stars. Sometimes the opening is also assisted by religious communities and their shared rituals, as well as the teachings of the religions, which at their best represent the distilled wisdom of the human race. In any case, we can never open the windows all by ourselves. One of the illusions of consumerism is that we can do things on our own and all by ourselves, without any help from others. In fact, we need the breathings of the universe and the Breathing of God as it breathes through the breathings. When these windows are opened—even for a moment—we breathe freely and feel more fully alive. The alternative to consumerism is this aliveness. Christians call it abundant living. Buddhists call it enlightenment. I call it practicing the presence of God.

As explained in the prologue, I use three sources to help me interpret this practice: process theology, Buddhism, and contemplative Christianity. In the remainder of this introduction I want to explain these three sources and, along the way, tell you a bit about my own spiritual pilgrimage. Then I will offer a special word to the skeptic, who may be interested in spirituality but may not necessarily believe in God. And finally, I will outline the chapters that follow, encouraging you to read them in whatever order you wish. The remainder of this introduction is devoted to these aims.

One Person's Journey

When people ask me about my religion, I sometimes say, "I am a Christian influenced by Buddhism." Often they look confused, because they are accustomed to thinking that if you are affiliated with one religion, you cannot learn from another. I am trying to say two things with my answer.

In the first place, I am trying to say that I am drawn to Christ, more than to anyone else, as my way to God. I am saying that I would like to live my life, day by day and moment by moment, in a way that "lives and dies daily" with him; that is, in sympathetic conformity to the inner feelings—the wisdom, compassion, and freedom—that filled his heart. And I am saying that in some deep and mysterious way, he continues to live, even after his death, as a healing presence in my life.

In the second place, I am trying to say that, as I see it, "living and dying daily" with Christ invites and even requires openness to truth wherever it is found, including other religions. This is because, for us Christians, "the Spirit of Christ" is not limited to Jesus. To be sure, the word *Christ* names a Jewish healer who walked the hills of Galilee some two thousand years ago and who died a painful death. It names Jesus. But it also names the creative and healing Spirit of God at work in the world. In the gospel of John this Spirit is called "the Logos." When I speak of God's Spirit or the Breath of Life in this book, I am speaking of this Logos.

To be sure, we Christians believe that this Logos was enfleshed or made visible in Jesus. We see it in his healing ministry, his forgiveness, his service to the poor, his fellowship with sinners and outcasts, his death, and his appearance to his disciples after that death. All these events reveal God to us. But we do not believe that God's Breathing was exhausted by these events. We believe that the Logos preceded Jesus' life and that it continued to exist after he died. Indeed, we believe that, after his death, his own heart became one with the Breathing, one with the Spirit. He became "the living Christ."

This means that whenever and wherever we see wisdom, compassion, and freedom in our world, even if only for a moment, we see God's Spirit. We see evidence of the living Christ. Given this perspective, it would be arrogant and even idolatrous for us to restrict "the Spirit of God" or "the living Christ" to believing Christians. In meeting another person in whom wisdom, compassion, and freedom are present, it would be idolatrous to say, "Sorry, but the Spirit of God, as manifest in Jesus, is restricted to people who think and feel like me." It would be much more honest to say, "In you I sense the very Spirit—the very Logos—that was manifest in Jesus. Let us learn from each other and be transformed by each other. There is more to God than I realized."

Of course, many of my fellow Christians do not take this attitude. Many have been taught that, if they are to be obedient to Christ, they must shut out other religions. They are skeptical when I say, "I am a Christian influenced by Buddhism." So I add, "It's kind of like being a Quaker."

This usually helps. They realize that, just as Quakers seek God in silent listening, so I seek God in silent listening. I then explain that I have found Buddhist meditation a tremendous help in becoming a better listener. The Protestant Christianity in which I was raised was pretty good at finding God in sound, but not so good at finding God in silence. From Buddhism we can learn that one of God's deepest languages is silence.

I hope this gives you, my reader, a provisional feel for what kind of Christian I am. I am a Christian influenced by Buddhism, who believes that the creative and healing Spirit of God in the world—the Spirit of Christ—is not limited to Christianity.

Of course, I am also much more than a "Christian influenced by Buddhism." I am a middle-class husband and father of two children; a professor of world religions at a small, liberal arts college; a member of a local United Methodist church; a communicant in a local Episcopal church; and a facilitator of a small group of Zen meditators—some Buddhist and some Christian—who meet regularly at that church for an hour of quiet sitting in Zen style.

In all these contexts I struggle with the realities of consumer culture. I struggle at home as my family and I wrestle with questions such as "How much is enough?" I struggle at work as I realize that my colleagues and I often place too much emphasis on three values of consumer culture—appearance, affluence, and achievement—and not enough emphasis on truth and service to the common good. And I struggle in church and in the Zen-meditation group as I realize how we, Christians and Buddhists alike, so often fall short of the simplicity and kindness to which Christianity and Buddhism point, each in different ways.

One reason that I am Christian, then, is that I would like to follow Christ more than I do. Although most middle-class Christians do not look to Buddhism, many of us are in a similar situation with respect to consumerism. Deep down, they—we—know that our middle-class lifestyles are too busy and too cluttered with "things" and that we fall short of the simpler living to which Christ calls us. We want to follow Christ, or at least we want to want to follow Christ. But our lives have not caught up with our better intentions. At best, we are but Christians in the making.

Ecotheology

Professionally, however, I am best known as an ecotheologian. I have written three books in the area of "ecological theology" and have edited two others. Like others who write in this area, I have wanted to show how the biosphere and its web of life can be a context for Christian self-understanding. I have wanted to describe a green Christianity.

My desire to envision this kind of Christianity is partly ethical. Historically, we Christians have so focused on human-divine relations and human-human relations that we have forgotten human-Earth relations and human-animal relations. We have too often neglected numerous responsibilities:

- To protect the habitats of wild plants and animals, whose species are now depleted at the rate of one species an hour
- To protect individual animals from cruelty and abuse, including those animals reared for food and subjected to scientific testing
- To curb forms of economic development that displace habitats and cause harm to individual animals
- To curb population, since the planet already contains too many people, given the needs of other creatures to flourish
- To live simply and frugally, thus preserving resources for future generations
- To restrict technologies that threaten the limits of the Earth to absorb pollution of atmosphere, water, and land

Unfortunately, I can count on one hand the number of sermons I have heard that addressed these issues. In this neglect, the Christian communities with which I am associated have forgotten many biblical themes: (1) that the plants and animals are declared by God to be good in their own right, quite apart from their usefulness to humans; (2) that it is the whole of creation, not human life alone, that God declares "very good"; (3) that the animals are themselves commanded by God to "be fruitful and multiply," a commandment that is never negated in the Bible; and (4) that, according to Paul in Romans, it is the whole of creation, not human life alone, that awaits redemption at the end of time. It is time that we remember these things and learn to live more lightly and compassionately on the Earth.

Thomas Berry is right. The Great Work of our time is not only to be happy and whole as individuals, doing personal work that is of service to others; it is also to help build communities that involve *mutually enhancing relations* between human beings and the rest of the Earth community.[7] I have become an ecotheologian because I have hoped that Christians might contribute to this Great Work before it is too late. For some species and for many individual animals, it is already too late. For Christians, the Great Work also involves confession and repentance: a profound recognition of how absent the Earth has been from our deeper concerns and of how many creatures have suffered in the process.

As with Thomas Berry, my desire to envision a green Christianity has been more than ethical. It has also been spiritual, although "spirituality" and "ethics" ought not to be sharply separated. I have been interested not only in how the Earth needs us to be good stewards but also in how we need the Earth to find God's Spirit in our individual and collective lives. As a young boy growing up in south Texas, my own soul was nourished not only by family and friends but also by rivers and dogs, trees and grass. I found God in nature as well as in church. In one of my books, called *With Roots and Wings,* I coined the term *green grace* to name the way in which God reaches us through plants and animals, hills and rivers, trees and stars.[8]

In my own experiences of institutional Christianity, green grace was not adequately recognized. To be sure, in the early days of Sunday school, we were able to talk about God's love for animals. We were invited to recognize that animals can be channels of grace, sacramental presences through which divine mystery is discovered. But somehow we were given the feeling that, as we grew older, we were to grow beyond such talk to move on to more serious matters, such as sin and redemption. People began to talk more about "red grace," the grace of Christ's blood on the cross, than about the "green grace" of rivers and dogs. By the time I was a teenager, religion seemed to be about human-human relations and human-divine relations, not human-Earth relations.

Process Theology

It was not until I attended seminary that I discovered a form of Christian theology, namely process theology, that seemed able to include grace both red and green. This is a form of Christian theology that emerged in the 1930s at the University of Chicago, is influenced by the cosmological perspective of Alfred North Whitehead, and has been adopted and developed by various Christian theologians, mostly Protestant, but some Catholic.

While Whitehead's perspective is a minority perspective within Western colleges and universities, it is something of a global movement. There is a European Center for Process Thought, a Japan Society for Process Studies, and a Whitehead Society of Korea, and there is an ongoing project in China to translate the works of Whitehead into Chinese. Most people who are influenced by Whitehead and by process theology believe that it has much to offer a world now fragmented by violence, poverty, and environmental destruction.

The process theology that I learned many years ago, and to which I have contributed over the years, taught that we humans belong not only to ourselves, and not only to one another, but also to a larger whole: to the web of life itself. It said that the other creatures in this web—the plants and the animals, the spirits and the ancestors—had value in and of themselves and that we could share in their feelings. And it said that this larger whole, the web of life, belongs to a still more inclusive whole, a Sacred Whole, who, like a very wise grandmother, loves each creature for its own sake, with a tender care that nothing be lost. This Sacred Whole is God. Understood in this way, God is both a personal presence to whom we can pray and an animating spirit within the whole of creation. In this book I will be drawing from this process understanding of God.

However, I do not speak of God as a Sacred Whole, as I did in my previous book, because this expression too often suggests that God is simply identical with the universe. Instead, as noted above, I speak of God as a "sky-like Mind" and "cosmic Womb" and "Open Space" within which the universe lives and moves and has its being. I hope these ways of speaking better explain what I intend to say and what is true to process theology: namely, that the universe is immanent within God but that God is also more than the universe.

This, then, is my fourth book in the area of process theology. The first three developed a process theology of ecology; here I develop a process theology of spirituality. More specifically, I develop a "process theology of spirituality" in dialogue with a "process theology of economics." This reveals the strong influence of my friend and teacher John B. Cobb, Jr.

Cobb was my teacher in seminary and then later in graduate school. When I studied with him, he was using process theology to interpret basic Christian beliefs about God, Christ, and the universe. Many of the theological positions of this book are indebted to Cobb's interpretations. In the intervening years, however, he began to use process thought as an aid in understanding contemporary economic realities. He began to realize that the function of theology is not only to interpret basic doctrines but also to address concrete social problems. In our time one of those problems is consumerism, or in Cobb's words, "economism."

Cobb's most systematic exposition of a "process" or "Whiteheadian" approach to economics occurs in *For the Common Good: Redirecting the Economy toward Community, the Environment, and a Sustainable Future,* which he co-authored with an environmental economist, Herman Daly.[9] In this book Cobb and Daly offer a detailed critique of contemporary economic theories, policies, and institutions, recommending alternatives in their stead. They point out that contemporary theories too often reduce people to isolated "consumers," neglecting the social and spiritual dimensions of our lives; and that these theories wrongly assume that the ever-increasing production and consumption of goods is an end in itself, without distinguishing healthy growth from unhealthy growth, and without recognizing that sometimes growth itself is undesirable. They ask and answer a basic question that is central to our time: What would economic theories, policies, and institutions look like if they took as their aim the promotion of human community in an ecologically responsible context, rather than ever-increasing economic growth?

The alternative that Daly and Cobb recommend is not bureaucratic socialism. Rather, it is a community-based market economy in which locally owned businesses supply goods and services to their con-stituencies; in which larger corporations are held accountable for the ways they affect communities; in which trade between nations is reserved for non-essential goods, with nations striving for self-reliance in terms of energy and agriculture; and in which the limits of the Earth to supply resources and absorb pollution are respected. They call this alternative way of thinking "economics for community."[10]

Of course, this is a work on spirituality, not economics. I lack the talent to advance the work of Cobb and Daly on economic theories, policies, and institutions. Still, I do not think we can talk about our capacities to be available to God's Breathing, individually and collectively, without talking about the tremendous influence of growth-based economics on our lives. In this book, then, I hope to make a small contribution to the prospects of an "economics for community" by describing certain aspects of a healthy spirituality that might help free us from the worst aspects of consumer culture, thus enabling us to live more abundantly. A post-consumer world will need social, economic, political, and spiritual foundations. I am trying to name some of the spiritual foundations.

Buddhism

The second influence for this book—Zen Buddhism—also emerged in seminary. When I was a senior in college, I embraced a very fundamentalist form of Christianity by which I tried to box in the world and God. I was quite sure that I was right about all doctrinal matters and that other people were wrong. I was equally sure that people of other religions—Buddhists, for example—were missing the boat.

By the time I arrived in seminary, I did not like the person I had become. I had thought that in becoming a Christian I would be more kind and gentle. Unfortunately, I was becoming more dogmatic and arrogant. In seminary, then, I was searching for a more open way of being Christian, a way that could be true to the Christian path, yet open to other religions. It was at this time that I discovered the writings of the late Trappist monk Thomas Merton, who became, through those writings, a spiritual mentor.

In particular, two books by Merton—*Contemplative Prayer* and *Mystics and Zen Masters*[11]—were helpful. The first introduced me to a way of praying without words and feelings, of praying in pure silence, where you rest in the freedom of listening itself, understood as a way of being present to God. The second book introduced me to Zen Buddhism, a way of entering into this silence and then living it out in the concrete activities of daily life.

About the time I was reading Merton, I was also taking courses in Buddhism at a local college. One day my Buddhism teacher called me on the phone and asked me if I would be willing to tutor for a year a Zen Buddhist monk from Japan, who was coming to the area to brush up on his English. With fear and trepidation, I agreed. For one full year, I served as his tutor, teaching him English by getting him to tell me about Zen. More directly than Merton, he introduced me to Zen, without the slightest hint that I need abandon my Christian path. I became, and still am, a "Zen-influenced Christian."

You, my reader, will undoubtedly detect the role of Buddhism in this book. You will hear it in my respect for "silence" as a way of being open to the world and to God; in my emphasis on spirituality as involving being wide awake moment by moment; in my emphasis on letting go of things when they pass away; in my recognition of the interdependence of all things, and in my suggestion that God's presence in our lives is analogous to physical breathing itself: rhythmic, nourishing, trustworthy, yet ungraspable.

Of course, many Buddhists do not speak of God. Still, I have found the Buddhist attention to breathing a helpful way of understanding the God in whom I believe. Accordingly, I find it helpful to speak of God's presence in the world as a cosmic "Breathing." I suspect that our own physical breathing, simple as it is, is one very important way of participating in this cosmic Breathing, which is holy and divine.

Contemplative Christianity

In addition to process theology and Buddhism, however, there is still a third source for this book. It is the contemplative tradition within Christian spirituality as introduced to me in a two-year course in spiritual direction that I took at the Shalem Institute for Spiritual Formation in Washington, D.C.

As a college teacher I often find myself talking with students about life situations and personal problems. Some of these students have been battling with depression, others with questions of sexual identity, others with problems of substance abuse, and still others with problems involving family and friends. The students will come to my office, and, for a short time, I will simply listen and care. I will describe one such student in chapter 3.

When students first came to see me early in my teaching career, I thought I was supposed to be in the business of problem solving. I felt like a failure if I wasn't able to give them practical advice that would help them move on with their lives and leave suffering and doubt behind. But gradually I came to realize two things. First, I really couldn't solve their problems, even if I wanted to, because I lacked the skill and training of a counselor. And, second, I didn't even feel called to solve their problems, because problem solving was not what I was about.

What I was about, I felt, was listening to them in a special way. I wanted to listen to that dimension of their lives—the spiritual dimension—in which God was already breathing in them, even if they didn't know it or think of it that way. Influenced by process theology and Buddhism, I trusted that God was in all the students who entered my office, guiding them toward that form of wholeness that was possible and available to them at that time in their lives; and that my task, as a teacher, was to help them hear that inner guidance, in their own ways and on their own terms. So I wasn't really trying to hear them into speech, but rather to hear them into listening. My experience was that, if I myself truly listened to them, in light of my sense that God was in them already, they might themselves become better listeners—listening not to me, but to a deeper teacher, an Inner Teacher, which was the breath of God itself.

As this interest in "listening to help others listen" emerged, I had no name for it. But I knew that this listening was different from problem solving and that, when I lapsed into the latter, I often lost the former. Through fortuitous and providential circumstances, I discovered friends who were experienced in something called "spiritual direction." I had never really heard of such direction, and I didn't like the sound of "directing" people, because it sounded too manipulative. But as these friends described what they meant by "spiritual direction," it sounded more and more like the kind of "listening" I felt called to. Indeed, some called it "holy listening."

One friend told me about a program at the Shalem Institute for Spiritual Formation that would introduce people to the tradition of holy listening in Christianity and also help them to be better holy listeners themselves. I enrolled in the program, took the two-year course, and received rewards I never imagined. Some of these rewards were quite personal. The Shalem program helped me discover forms of prayer and discernment that were right for me and that helped me better understand the spiritual dimension of my own life. It also helped me, I believe, to be a better spiritual friend, or holy listener, to the people who crossed my path.

But some of the lessons were more academic. First, the Shalem program helped outline and categorize the issues that are important to people interested in the spiritual dimension of religious life. And second, the Shalem program helped introduce me to many writings, contemporary and historical, that address those issues.

As a Protestant seminarian, I had never really learned very much about the history of Christian spirituality. My training focused on the first two dimensions of religious life, intellectual understanding and compassionate action, at the expense of the third, spiritual depth. I had never read the works of the Desert Fathers and Mothers, John of the Cross, Teresa of Avila, Brother Lawrence, the Quakers, Julian of Norwich. Even after I had completed a Ph.D. in philosophy of religion and theology, I was still largely ignorant of the history of Christian spirituality, save what I had learned indirectly through the writings of Thomas Merton.

The program at Shalem helped change this. It introduced me to traditions of mysticism and prayer, discernment and spiritual direction that I never knew existed. I realized that Christianity has a long and rich spiritual heritage and that I had much to learn from it.

In this book I cannot claim to draw extensively from that heritage. There is too much of it, and I am still but a learner. But I will be drawing from selected traditions within it, sometimes explicitly and often implicitly. I am grateful to the people at Shalem for introducing me to these sources.

Even though these various sources are important to me, I do not write this book in order to make you a process theologian, a Buddhist, or a contemplative. The ideas that I present can stand on their own for your judgment; you need not embrace my sources in order to evaluate, and perhaps also learn from, the ideas. What is important is that, in some small way, the ideas take you and me alike beyond ideas to the realm of God's Breathing. After all, this is the purpose of life. It is not to have the right ideas or names. It is to breathe deeply.

Welcoming the Skeptic

As I write this book, I am hoping that you, my reader, are already disposed to believe in God and trust in God's Breathing, however you might name it. I trust that you have been breathed by the Breathing amid the beauty of nature, the mystery of music, the creativity of fresh thinking, the intimacies of personal relationships, and the courage with which you have faced difficult times. I am interested in helping you and me alike recognize the wisdom, the pure grace that is available to us within ordinary life.

But I also recognize that some among my readers might be more skeptical. Perhaps you have been overwhelmed with tragedy in life and cannot reconcile the existence of divine Freshness with the reality of unspeakable sadness. Perhaps you have been burdened by an overly authoritarian view of God—say that of a Policeman-in-the-Sky—and cannot imagine God in any other way. Or perhaps you are deeply impressed with the wisdom of modern science and cannot reconcile the wisdom of science with what sometimes seems like the "blind faith" of religion. If you are among the skeptics, I have two things to say to you.

First, I hope you keep reading. My aim is not to persuade you to believe in God and God's Breathing if you are disposed otherwise. It is best to be true to the best of your lights, even if this involves doubt concerning God and God's Breathing. My aim is to suggest ways in which you might already experience this Breathing even if you do not believe in God. Of course, I do hope that my discussions of experience might make belief in Open Space more plausible to you. If you end up believing in God after reading this book, I say, "Good." In order to be open to the Breathing of the Open Space, it can help to believe in it.

Nevertheless, you do not have to believe in the Open Space in order to touch and taste its healing presence. You do not have to believe in the ocean in order to be washed by its clear waters. The ocean offers the same cleanliness for everyone. There are ways of being washed that have nothing to do with formal religious belief. You can be spiritual without being religious and without being theistic.

Second, I offer a word of advice on how you might read the book. You might want to turn to chapter 6, where I introduce the worldview of process theology. Then you will understand more clearly the cosmological perspective I bring to this work. What my own experience suggests is that Whitehead's perspective offers three things that may speak to some of your doubts.

First, Whitehead seeks to make sense of God in light of what we know from modern science, particularly evolutionary theory, quantum theory, and chaos theory. Many people feel that, if we are open to the wisdom of science, we must be closed to the wisdom of spirituality. Whitehead suggests the contrary, and I do, too. With him I suggest that the more open we are to science at its frontiers, the more plausible it becomes to speak of an Open Space and its Breathing. Science tells us that the universe began some fifteen billion years ago with a primal flaring forth, from which emerged the stars and the galaxies in various generations, and then, very late in our galaxy, our own small planet with its myriad forms of life. It tells us that this ongoing process has contained a certain kind of creativity, such that, if we rewound the history of the universe and started anew with the same initial conditions, the new version might unfold very differently, with different forms of life or no life at all.

From the perspective of Whitehead, this creative process has occurred within an Open Space that is filled with many possibilities and that functions as a cosmic lure—a lure toward novelty and order—within the nature of things. We see evidence of this lure in the emergence of atoms out of subatomic particles, gases out of atoms, stars out of gases, and galaxies out of stars. In life on Earth we see it in the emergence of cells out of molecules, tissues out of cells, organs out of tissues, multi-celled organisms out of single-celled organisms. The lure is also present as a lure toward chaos, toward disorder, when existing forms of order have grown stale. This cosmic lure is the divine Breathing. It operates throughout nature in a quiet and patient way, and it also operates within human life as a lure toward spiritual depth. It is that within each of us that makes us want to be washed of our greed, hatred, and envy and become more wise, compassionate, and free in our daily lives.

Second, Whitehead rejects images of God that overemphasize judgment at the expense of love. To be sure, there is a time for judgment in our lives. When people kill other people in violent ways, we rightly say, "That is bad." When innocent people die terrible deaths, we rightly say, "That is horrible." When greedy people have far too much money, while others suffer from severe poverty, we rightly say, "That is unfair." And when we ourselves fall into greed, hatred, and illusion, we rightly say, "I have done wrong." There is a place in life for judging other people's actions, outer circumstances, and ourselves. But much Western religion has so overemphasized the theme of judgment that many people now feel that they've had an overdose. When they hear the word *God*, all they hear is "A Policeman in the Sky." They do not hear The Freshness Deep Down or The Luckiness of Being. They cannot hear Open Space. In Whitehead's view, this is because early Christians too easily projected onto life's Mystery the image of a powerful political ruler. They rendered unto God what belongs to Caesar.

Third, Whitehead's perspective offers a way of thinking about God that has helped many people trust in the Freshness even as they lament and resist the many tragedies of life. Whitehead believes that the universe is a communion of subjects, not a collection of objects, and that each subject in this universe—from the smallest atom to the largest star—is filled with a creativity that can "breathe with" or "breathe against" the divine Breathing. The creatures are free. The divine Breathing, to which they may or may not respond in their freedom, originates from an Open Space within which the communion occurs.

Here, perhaps, traditional Christian language is helpful, even if you are not Christian. You might think of the Open Space as "God the Father" and the Breathing as "the Holy Spirit." I will say more about the third person of this Trinity—namely, Jesus—in chapters to come. The point here is simply that the Breathing of the Open Space—the guidance of the Holy Spirit—is always present within creation, but that it is, of necessity, persuasive rather than coercive, creative but not controlling, healing and not manipulating. There are some things that happen in life—unspeakable tragedies, for example—that arise from the creativity of various creatures in the universe and that even the Breathing cannot prevent. Heal? Yes. Prevent? No. As I write this book, I do presuppose the reality of God, but I do not believe that God is all-powerful in the sense of "being able to do anything God wishes."

Perhaps these considerations incline you to be slightly more sympathetic to the perspective of this book. In any case, let me emphasize that it is not really necessary to agree with this way of understanding God, or even to believe in God at all, in order to read and agree with much of this book. The various ways of being breathed by God that I present in this book—discernment and delight in beauty, for example—are trans-theological. They can be appreciated by people who understand God differently than I do, and they can be appreciated by people who do not believe in God. My concern in this book is primarily with religious experience, not religious belief. It is with practicing the presence of God in an age of consumerism, not with believing in the God whose presence is practiced.

Reading the Rest of this Book

The remainder of this book consists of six chapters and a conclusion. Chapter 1 is an introduction to spirituality, or living from the Center. It names and defines nine ways that we can know God in daily life: (1) discernment, (2) sacramental awareness, (3) openness to healing, (4) living-by-dying, (5) trust in open space, (6) deep listening, (7) courage in suffering, (8) creativity, and (9) loving-kindness, which includes delight in beauty and intimacy with others. This chapter also proposes that there are three dimensions to religious life: intellectual understanding, practical action, and spiritual depth; and it takes note of three problems that emerge in human life when depth is neglected: fundamentalism, burnout, and the will-to-power. The chapter simultaneously introduces the problem of consumerism and discusses the way in which, in consumer society, spirituality is often absorbed into the will-to-power or its psychological correlate, spiritual narcissism. If there is a single chapter that provides an overview of the many topics addressed in this book, chapter 1 is that chapter.

Chapter 2 is a more extensive discussion of consumer society, taking note of the ten temptations of consumerism and presenting the theology of consumerism. The chapter simultaneously presents in more detail two of the nine ways of experiencing God, discernment and sacramental awareness, suggesting that discernment is needed if we are to avoid the ten temptations of consumerism and live more spiritually. In the latter context it recommends five guidelines for discernment, based on process theology. The chapter includes a discussion of "the Budweiser Christian," who wrongly approaches the whole of life, and even God, in the spirit of the Budweiser advertisement that says "This Bud's for You." It closes with an image of Jesus at the mall and with a constructive proposal that his rebirth occurs when all of us, each in our own way, transcend the Budweiser mentality and open ourselves to the deeper Breathing of God. This chapter offers the most systematic interpretation of consumerism offered in the book.

Chapter 3 turns to the subject of grace, or the "luckiness within life," and discusses the way in which the deeper happiness in life—the happiness that is beyond consumer-driven pleasure—comes by letting go into that grace, which lies within and beyond each of us. The chapter also includes a discussion of happiness in America, proposing (1) that there are three contexts for happiness in America: meaningful work, healthy personal relations, and leisure; (2) that true happiness is a byproduct, not a goal, of life; (3) that happiness is relative, not absolute; (4) that happiness, like envy, can be contagious; and (5) that the deeper happiness is living from the Center. The chapter closes with a practical recommendation of four steps all of us might take, each in our own way, to live from the Center and thus find the deeper happiness. These four steps are the most practical advice I offer in the book for "what to do" if we want to find spiritual depth in our lives.

Chapter 4 deals with three more of the nine ways of experiencing God in daily life: loving-kindness, living-by-dying, and deep listening or silence. In so doing I tell the story of my own fundamentalist period and suggest that the heart of fundamentalism lies in a fear of letting go of creeds and doctrines, even when they have become false gods in our lives. I propose that silence, as cultivated in Zen meditation, is one practice that can assist in this letting go, and that silence can simultaneously enable us to be more open and loving toward others, so that we can listen to them on their own terms and for their own sakes. The chapter also includes a discussion of another kind of false god, namely, the legitimate psychological need that has become a compulsion. I note nine needs that can easily become compulsions, including the needs to be perfect, to be in control, to always be happy. For readers facing problems of addiction, including addiction to perfectionism and flattery and busyness, this may be the most important of chapters.

Chapter 5 turns to two additional ways of experiencing God in daily life: courage in suffering, and faith—or, as I speak of it, "trust in Open Space." I suggest that faith is different from belief and that the intuitive, nonverbal content of faith includes four insights: (1) that there is more to life than our private suffering; (2) that there is grace sufficient to each moment; (3) that suffering and joys are shared by the very heart of the universe; and (4) that in the last analysis, all will be well. This chapter also deals with the problems of evil and suffering, briefly explaining the process approach to tragedy. For readers who wrestle deeply with the problem of evil and who wonder how faith in God is possible without hiding or running away from the sadder sides of life, this will be an important chapter.

Chapter 6 offers a more extensive explanation of the process, or Whiteheadian, worldview, explaining that it is one of many worldviews that can provide an intellectual alternative to the worldview of consumerism. The chapter also presents the ethical guidelines that follow from a process perspective, utilizing aspects of a document called the Earth Charter. For readers interested in the intellectual foundations and ethical implications of spirituality in the age of consumerism, this will be an especially important chapter. The earlier chapters emphasize "right breathing" in the age of consumerism. This chapter turns more directly to "right thinking" and "right acting" as a balance to our more intuitive awakenings to divine presence.

I hope that the book unfolds in a linear fashion, such that each chapter builds on and adds to its predecessors. Thus, if you seek an ordered presentation of ideas, it is best to read the book from first to last chapter. Nevertheless, as explained in the Prologue, you can freely read chapters in a more spontaneous way, turning to those that interest you. If you want to read in this way, you might turn to the Table of Contents and read sections that interest you. In reading this book, as in so many other aspects of life, the best guide is your own inner wisdom, which is itself one manifestation of God's Breathing.

CHAPTER ONE

When God Breathes

Spirituality as Living from the Center

*When he had said this, he breathed on them
and said to them, "Receive the Holy Spirit."*
John 20:22

*The whole aim of the Christian life is to be a Spirit-bearer,
to live in the Spirit of God, to breathe the Spirit of God.*
Kallistos Ware, The Orthodox Way[1]

*God is not far from each one of us, for "in God we live
and move and have our being."*
Acts 17:27–28

During my senior year in college, for about ten months, I was a Christian fundamentalist. I believed that God had a mouth without lungs, or, to be slightly more accurate, that God could speak but not breathe. God could make verbal pronouncements from the heavens, telling us how the world came into existence and offering us instructions on how to live. We could follow God's instructions by reading the Bible, which consisted of oral teachings in written form. But God could not really touch us or be touched by us in more intimate and non-doctrinal ways. We could obey God's teachings, so I thought, but we could not feel God's breathing.

Even as I believed in this faraway God, I secretly hoped and sometimes felt that God was more intimate. I sensed, but could not admit, that I myself had been breathed by God through the gentle presence of a crucified carpenter, the love and forgiveness of friends and family, the healing presence of plants and animals, the daily bread

35

of the dinner table, the joys and struggles of ordinary life, and the interior movements of my own soul. I sensed that God had been praying within me, and within all creatures, with sighs too deep for words.

Gradually, and with much struggle, I learned to accept these deeper feelings. With the help of a contemporary form of Christian theology called "process theology," I found a way to envision God not only as a personal presence to whom I could pray but also as a creative and healing spirit within plants and animals, trees and stars, souls and bodies. I began to think of God not so much as a male deity residing off the planet but as an Open Space—an opened heart—within which the entire universe unfolds, epoch by epoch and moment by moment. Paul's saying in Acts that God is a reality in which we live and move and have our being came to make sense to me. Paul and process theology helped me move past the idea that God was outside me and helped me see more deeply that I was inside God.

Other sources helped too. With the help of biblical scholars and Jewish storytellers, I came to realize that biblical stories can be poetically true without being historically factual. And with the help of various spiritual companions, many Christian but some Buddhist, I came to see that our most important connections with God are deeper than words can grasp. Today I feel quite grateful to all these helpers.

Nevertheless, when I first entered college teaching, I wasn't sure I had permission to honor the more intimate and nonverbal experiences of God. Somehow I had the impression that we theologians and philosophers were supposed to focus only on words and ideas, not on more immediate and direct experiences. And even when I did feel free to acknowledge the less discursive and more immediate side of religious life, I sometimes lacked the words to name God's nonverbal yet palpable presence. Several years ago, one of my students offered a name. She called it "God's Breathing." Her story is instructive.

Salvation from Self-Starvation

Five days a week, nine months a year, I teach world religions to college undergraduates. Often, on the first day of class, I ask my students to define "religion," and over the years a pattern of discussion has emerged.

One group of students will define religion as a function of the intellect. "Religion," they say, "is a set of convictions. It is believing certain things about God and the universe and purpose in life." Another group will then disagree, defining religion as a function of the will. "That's too intellectual," they will say. "Religion is not what people believe; it's what they do. It's going to church and worshiping at temples and giving to the poor."

For a moment, it will seem as if a choice must be made between religion-as-belief and religion-as-behavior, but then synthesis will be reached. "We are both right," they will conclude. "Religion is believing certain things and then acting on those beliefs. It is applied belief."

As this is said, a third group of students, more soft-spoken and introspective, will seem troubled. They will agree that religion includes personal belief and outward behavior. But they will also sense that, in religion at its deepest and best, something more is involved.

One year a young woman—the one I mentioned above—put it this way: "For me, religion has a deeper dimension, a spiritual dimension. It is not just about believing the right things and acting in the right ways; it's also about being breathed by God, moment by moment, day by day, whether you are in heaven or in hell. It's about God's Breathing."

As she spoke, many of her fellow students looked perplexed. The skeptics among them weren't sure there was a God in the first place; the believers weren't sure God could breathe; and no one was sure what it meant to be breathed by God in hell. But I knew what she meant. For one thing, I knew that in the Bible the very concept of God's Spirit comes from the Hebrew word *ruah,* meaning "wind" or "breath." I knew that, for her, "God's Breathing" referred to what Christians call "the Spirit of God" or "the Breath of Life" or "the Holy Spirit." For another, I knew her story. I knew that she had herself been been to hell and that it was by God's Breathing that she'd been saved.

In high school, so I realized, she had tried to starve herself. Her hell had been anorexia. For three years, from ages fifteen to eighteen, she had weighed only ninety pounds. In sheer desperation and on the verge of suicide, she had turned to religion—in her case, Christianity—as a source of power and self-esteem. She started praying and going to church; and she joined a small group at the church for people with eating disorders. It wasn't just a set of beliefs she was looking for or a code of conduct. It was fresh energy and courage and hope. It was God.

"And I found God," she said. "God was a still small voice within me who told me that life was worth living, when suicide seemed a more plausible alternative. God was the love that I received from friends and family, even when I felt myself totally unworthy. And God was the courage that I found to eat again, even when my stomach was so shrunken that digesting even one bite would be painful."

This, then, is what she meant by God's Breathing. She meant a healing and whole-making Spirit at work in others and in herself, through which she had found new life. She was suggesting that the world's religions at their best are not just products of human belief and human action. They are ways of being available to God's Breathing.

Living from the Center

Let us assume with my student that there really is this Breathing in our world. Let us assume that the energy of the universe is not limited to the energy understood by physics and chemistry, but that it also includes a creative and healing spirit—a divine Breathing—that is around us and within us, if we can somehow manage to be open to it.

My student's story illustrates just how desperately we can need this Breathing amid our own personal hells. Her hell was an inner addiction to being thin. It was shaped by a certain image she had seen on television countless times: that of a beautiful woman, admired by men, with a perfectly thin body. Our hells may be different. We may be inwardly addicted to being perfect, being needed, receiving the approval of others, being in control, or being successful by the standards of consumer culture. In some circumstances these needs are natural and good. It is fine to want a pleasing appearance, to want enough money to pay the rent, and to feel satisfaction in a job well done. But when appearance, affluence, and achievement become the central organizing principles of our lives, and thus compulsions, we are enslaved. Our natural needs have become unnatural compulsions, and they become false gods. This is the seduction of consumerism. It elevates finite needs, which are natural in some circumstance, into infinite goods. It encourages what Christianity calls "inordinate attachment."

Often, we do not realize that our finite needs have become false gods until a crisis occurs. Something happens in our lives and we are forced to wake up. Despite our compulsion to be perfect, we fail miserably; despite our compulsion to be needed, others do not need us; despite our compulsion to receive approval, people don't like us; despite our compulsion to be in control, things fall apart; despite our compulsion to succeed, we fail. When these things happen, we must then find a source of wisdom, compassion, and inner freedom that helps us get past these hells and find new life. We must find God's Breathing.

One danger, of course, is that we will not be prepared for these crises because we have not been attentive to God's Breathing in our lives. It is a little like needing to parachute from a plane that is crashing, but having never learned to parachute. Sometimes, for some of us, it is too late. We have a nervous breakdown, fall into depression, or lash out at others as if it were "their" fault. We fall apart.

Still another danger is that, even if we successfully parachute, we fall back into the old ways once the crisis passes. This is the way it is with so many addictions. The alcoholic does something terrible, repents of his sins, seeks the forgiveness of others, but then drinks again. His need, and ours as well, is for a way of living, day by day and moment by moment, in which the temptations can be resisted and he can get on with the business of life, which is to live wisely, compassionately, and freely in service to others. His need is for what Quaker Thomas Kelly calls continuously renewed immediacy.[2] God's Breathing is this immediacy.

What name shall we give to this life of continuously renewed immediacy? In the Introduction I called it practicing the presence of God; here, following Thomas Kelly, let me call it living from the Center.

In *A Testament of Devotion*, Kelly describes people who live from this Center. They may be clerks or plumbers, nurses or teachers, artists or homemakers, grandmothers or young children. Whatever their station in life, they have an inner joy, a freshness in their actions, a healing presence before others, and a capacity to say yes and no with confidence. They are free from internal distractions and thus available to each situation in ways that are fitting: laughing with those who need laughter, crying with those who need tears, and being quiet with those who need silence. They feel deeply connected with others, yet they are not afraid to be alone. They are active in the world, yet their actions are not fueled by nervous energy or the will-to-mastery. They live from a deeper place, an inner place, a more prayerful place. They have spiritual depth.[3]

But let me be honest. Most of us, myself much included, enter into this depth only in our better moments. A baby is born, a loved one dies, a friend needs help, a crisis needs mending—and we rise to the occasion. But then, a day or two later, we are breathless and uncentered, like prodigal sons and daughters who have wandered from the Breathing. If sainthood means living from the Center, then most of us are but momentary saints. Often we are struggling.

The Problem of Spiritual Narcissism

Why do we struggle so much? There are many reasons, some of them beyond our control. Our chemistry may be out of balance, our hearts may be broken. In subsequent chapters I will suggest that one of the reasons we struggle is that we are held captive by an unhealthy yet corporate-sponsored world religion, which I call consumerism. Perhaps one reason has to do with the tendency in non-consumerist religions—otherwise called traditional religions—to reduce religion to the practical application of fervently held belief at the expense of spirituality.

Recall the thesis of my student. She suggested that a healthy religious life has three dimensions: intellectual understanding, practical action, and spiritual depth. We might call them "right thinking" and "right acting" and "right breathing." And she intimated that when the third dimension is neglected, something is missing.

It seems to me that she is right. It seems that when religion is reduced to applied belief, three problems often emerge, all of which are obstacles to spirituality, but all of which can be healed by attention to the spiritual dimension of human life.

The first problem is "fundamentalism." This arises when we are so attached to our own personal beliefs, liberal or conservative, that we reduce God to our concept of God and life to our concept of life. We then walk through life with mental grids into which we try to fit all people and all experiences, at the expense of recognizing the mystery of life and the mystery of God. We forget that Truth is more than our concept of truth.

A second problem is "burnout." This occurs when we are so attached to our goals for practical action that we assume that, if these goals are not met, our lives will amount to nothing. We then invest so much energy in trying to meet our goals that the goals themselves become our gods. When our best-laid plans break down, and the future does not unfold as we wish, we grow weary and cynical. The world has not been worth our effort.

A third problem is "will-to-mastery." This occurs when we unconsciously try to remake the world in our own image, often under the auspices of "trying to help others." Often this willful impulse occurs in association with fundamentalism or activism. We try to remake the world either by having others believe as we believe or by trying to make them behave as we behave. Or at least as we think we ought to behave.

Of course, there are times when influencing the world in such ways is good. It is good to encourage others to transcend their greed, hatred, and envy; and it is good when they try to encourage us as well. There is an important place in life for mutual edification through word and deed. This occurred in the life of my student. At one stage in her illness, a good friend walked up to her and said, "You are sick and you need help." Her friend was trying to influence her. The friend's will-to-influence was an act of love.

The problem emerges when our desire to influence and edify others becomes a desire to control them completely. Then the "others" whom we are trying to influence become objects we try to master rather than subjects whom we truly love. Our will-to-help becomes a will-to-mastery.

Unfortunately, this temptation toward mastery is compounded by the cultural ethos of our time, namely consumerism. One aspect of consumerism is its tendency to reduce all things into commodities for purchase in the marketplace. This reduction of the world to "mere objects" has implications for spirituality.

Consider the words of George Soros, a billionaire financier. He writes that "markets reduce everything, including human beings (labor) and nature (land) to commodities." He accepts this fact about markets, but laments that contemporary society easily becomes absorbed into this commodifying mindset. "We can have a market economy," he says, "but we cannot have a market society."[4]

The problem, however, is that we do have a market society. We have a society in which market-based values define the atmosphere in which we live and move and have our being. To the degree that we are dominated by these values, we easily and unwittingly reduce "spiritual disciplines" such as prayer or meditation into technologies for "giving us good feelings" or "making ourselves happy." And we reduce God's Spirit to a commodity we hope to hold in standing reserve. In this way, a legitimate search for spiritual depth devolves into spiritual materialism. All things, even holy things, become commodities.

The other side of this materialism is narcissism. When we are shaped by the ideal that "We Can Have It All," our own egos become the central organizing principle of our spiritual lives. It is as if the world were a vast solar system and our small selves the sun. We then approach other people and the surrounding world as if their very purpose were to orbit our lives or, to use common parlance, "to meet our needs." Even God becomes a planet.

From the perspective of this book, God is not a planet. Rather, God is an Open Space within which all real planets live and move and have their being. We ourselves are among the planets that dwell in this Open Space. Moreover, this Open Space is an opened heart. It breathes in us and around us, all the time, in a creative and healing way. Our task is to be available to this Breathing.

The life of continuously renewed immediacy—of living from the Center—always has two sides: a human side and a divine side.

The human side consists in our being open or available to the Breathing, so that it can nourish and guide our lives. This cooperation can be conscious or unconscious, intentional or unintentional. A loved one dies, a baby is born, a marriage occurs, a task needs performing—and consciously or unconsciously, intentionally or unintentionally, something goes wide in our hearts. The widening is part of what I mean by availability. It is a letting go of things that bind us, so that we can live from the deeper Center.

The divine side lies in the influence of the Spirit consequent to our "going wide." This influence is not one-sided or unilateral. It is not that we empty ourselves of all creativity so that God's creativity can then do all the work. Rather, it is that we empty ourselves of a false creativity—a creativity based on our private ego—so that we can cooperate with a deeper creativity that is wise, compassionate, and free. Something goes wide in our hearts, and we find ourselves even more creative, in wise and compassionate ways, than we were beforehand.

The greater creativity belongs to God and to us. It is God working in us and us working in God. We become God's hands, God's eyes, God's ears, God's body. Our own lives, our own breathing, can then become a context in which others receive and awaken to the Breathing. For the moment, at least, we are at one with God. We are breathed by the Breathing.

Envisioning the God Who Breathes

At this point it may be helpful to explain more carefully what I mean by "God" and "God's Breathing." By now it should be clear that when I say that God breathes, I do not mean that the infinite Mystery at the heart of the universe has a self-enclosed body with lungs. I am not proposing, as my young son once put it, that "God looks like Colonel Sanders." To the best of my knowledge, the only body that God has on an ongoing basis is the universe itself, with its galaxies and stars, hills and rivers, plants and animals, spirits and ancestors, sinners and saints, joys and sufferings. To this vast and unfolding cosmos, we need not add an additional body, located in space, that looks like Colonel Sanders. The universe is body enough.

Still, I recommend five ideas that come from process theology, which is the theological perspective undergirding this work. They are:

- That the universe unfolds within the larger environment of an infinite Clearing—an Open Space—that is a receptacle for all its happenings
- That this Open Space is not an empty vacuum, but rather a sky-like Mind filled with wisdom, compassion, and freedom
- That in its compassion, this sky-like Mind is not simply interested in the general welfare of the universe, but that it also shares in the joys and suffering of each creature, on its own terms and for its own sake
- That this sky-like Mind is also within each creature, at each and every moment of its life, beckoning that creature toward the fullness of life, relative to what is possible for it in the situation at hand
- That this Lure, itself present within each human heart, is also present throughout the unfolding of the cosmos, as the very Lure by which the molecules emerged from atoms, living cells from molecules, plants and animals from living cells

God, then, is my name for the sky-like Mind by which the universe has been called into being over billions of years of evolution. And *Breathing* is my metaphor for the way in which this Mind can enlighten our minds, lighten our loads, widen our hearts, animate our wills, and provide us with fresh possibilities in daily life.

The last idea named above—that of the universe bearing witness to a cosmic Lure—is particularly important for a dialogue between religion and science. It suggests that the very history of the universe is best understood not simply as a purposeless unfolding of lifeless matter in motion but rather as creative response, by a universe that is itself creative, to the continuing influence of a sky-like Mind. For process theologians, such a view is not only more religiously meaningful, but also more scientifically adequate, since it takes into account (1) the nonmechanistic and creative nature of the universe, to which quantum physics and chaos theory now bear witness, and (2) the evident fact that, over vast periods of time, the universe itself has evolved fresh forms of order and consciousness, despite the tendencies of matter toward entropy. God, so process theologians suggest, is indeed that counterentropic Lure by which the universe has been evoked to create new forms of order and heightened capacities for consciousness, human and nonhuman alike.

Of course, this book is not the context to explore this dialogue with science in depth, a worthy endeavor that is best left for other works. Nevertheless, it remains important that God and God's Breathing are consistent with, not antagonistic to, what we learn from science in many of its forms and also what we learn from psychology, particularly humanistic and transpersonal psychologies. The Lure toward fresh forms of order and consciousness within the universe as a whole is itself also the Lure toward wholeness, including spiritual wholeness, within each living being. The idea, then, is that what we find when we look beyond ourselves is also what we find when we look within ourselves.

A God with Many Names

In the history of religions, this Breathing has been named in many ways. Christians speak of the *Spirit of God* or the *Holy Spirit* and the *Breath of Life*. We believe that it helped animate the universe into existence some fifteen billion years ago; that it is the breath of life within each living being on our planet; that it inspired the prophets of Hebrew Scripture; and that it was enfleshed, but not exhausted, in the healing ministry of Jesus. We trust that this Spirit is still present today as a source of comfort, guidance, and fresh revelation. Our aim is to be available to this Spirit, to be Spirit-bearers.

Still, we recognize—or ought to recognize—that the Spirit is not limited to Christianity or known only by Christians. For example, in Hinduism the Breathing is felt and known as *Shakti,* the female energy of God. Hindus feel this female energy in places of worship that are wide awake with vitality and energy, in the numinous energies of nature, and in the hearts of human beings when they are able to face suffering with deep courage.

In Taoism, to offer another example, the Breathing is sometimes called the *Tao.* Taoists feel the Tao as an invisible yet flowing energy that courses through the natural world and that can be part of one's own body in the form of vital energy, or *ch'i.* Both these traditions, and many others besides, can help enrich a Christian understanding of the Spirit. Each religion offers its own distinctive experience of the Spirit, which then complements and adds to the other religions. No religion has a monopoly on God's Breathing.

Of course, these different ways of naming and experiencing the Breathing can be challenging to many Christians. Certainly, they would have been challenging to me during my fundamentalist period. During this time I could not admit that God's Spirit might be named and felt in feminine terms, and I was not at all interested in the possibility that God might be present in other religions. I was pretty sure that God was male, that God was a Christian, and that this God was a lot like me.

Now I believe that I was wrong, as are other fundamentalists who reduce the Spirit to one religion. If we wrongly assume that there is but one name for the Breathing and one way for experiencing it, namely our own, we fall into idolatry. We make a god of our own words and experiences. In truth, God's Breathing is as different from the names we give it as fresh air is from the phrase "fresh air." Just as a person gasping for air cannot be saved by the word "air" but needs instead the real presence of real air, so a person gasping for God's Breathing cannot be saved by mere names for the Breathing. He or she needs the real presence of a living Spirit. This real presence transcends all our names for it, and it is always more than our experience of it. The real presence of God in our lives is more like a physical energy than like an abstract idea. It is the Breath of Life, which animates all living beings.

In my case I use the word *Breathing* rather than *Breath* because I want to stress that the actual presence of the divine spirit in our lives and in the universe is dynamic rather than static, flowing rather than fixed, rhythmic rather than reified. In this sense the Breathing is similar not only to fresh air but also to the process of breathing itself. Just as we cannot grasp our own breathing, but we can indeed be animated by it, so cannot grasp God's Breathing, but we can indeed be animated by it. This, I believe, is the very purpose of life. It is to be available to God's Breathing in each present moment.

In order to be available to this Breathing, it helps if we recognize it when it occurs. It helps to be able to look at our own lives and those of others and say, "Yes, I see God present in this way of living." Toward this end, I want to name nine ways of experiencing God—nine ways of practicing the presence of God, of living from the Center—that are found in the history of religion and ordinary life. In order to approach them, let us briefly shift from the metaphor of God's presence as a "breathing" that we inhale to God's presence as a "food" that we eat. I want to present nine ways of eating the bread of heaven.

The Bread of Heaven

Jesus himself had a thing about eating. Consider the following passages from the New Testament:

"For the bread of God is that which comes down from heaven and gives life to the world." They said to him, "Sir, give us this bread always." (Jn. 6:33–34)

"I am the living bread...Those who eat my flesh and drink my blood have eternal life...for my flesh is true food and my blood is true drink." (Jn. 6:51, 54, 55)

Then he ordered the crowds to sit down on the grass. Taking the five loaves and the two fish, he looked up to heaven, and blessed and broke the loaves, and gave them to the disciples, and the disciples gave them to the crowds. And all ate and were filled. (Mt. 14:19–20)

When they had gone ashore, they saw a charcoal fire there, with fish on it, and bread. Jesus said to them, "Come and have breakfast." (Jn. 21:9, 12)

For those of us who think of spirituality as abstract and ethereal, it is interesting that Jesus' metaphors are themselves so concrete and bodily. He compares God to bread that comes down from heaven giving life to the world; he invites his disciples to eat his own flesh; he takes five loaves of bread, divides them, and then distributes them among five thousand; and one of his first acts after his resurrection is to feed people breakfast. He seems to know that God can be known through the sharing and eating of food.

Many Christians can benefit from taking Jesus more seriously. They—we—too often reduce Christianity to the practical application of fervently held beliefs, falling into an overemphasis on beliefs or moral activity at the expense of more contemplative dimensions of the Christian life. As noted above, with our emphasis on applied belief we often forget that God can be experienced in more palpable and less doctrinal ways. Eating is one of the most palpable acts in which we participate on a daily basis, involving sight, touch, taste, and smell. If we cannot find God in the preparing and eating of food, and in sharing that food with others, it is likely that God is too abstract, that when we speak of God, we are really just talking about an idea in our heads. Jesus takes us out of our heads and into our bodies.

Interestingly, one of the leading interpreters of Christianity in the twentieth century, C. S. Lewis, takes the bodiliness of Christianity as part of its very essence. In *Mere Christianity* he says that Christianity is bodily in at least two ways. First, says Lewis, Christianity rightly recognizes that those in whom Christ truly dwells are bodily extensions of his own healing ministry, such that they are, as it were, his fingers and muscles. In Lewis' words,

> Let me make it quite clear that when Christians say the Christ-life is in them, they do not mean simply something mental or moral…They mean that Christ is actually operating through them; that the whole mass of Christians are the physical organism through which Christ acts—that we are his fingers and muscles, the cells of His Body.[5]

Elsewhere he compares this extension of his healing ministry to the catching of a healing and whole-making disease. We "put on the mind of Christ" and thus become infected, albeit in a loving way, with the very condition that Jesus himself embodied. It is as if we had caught a wondrous disease that gives us new life rather than death. This new life is the mind of Christ.

Second, Christianity is bodily in the sense that it says we can receive Christ—we can internalize the spirit of God—not only by mental acts of belief, but also by more bodily rituals, such as the water of baptism and the sacrament of communion. We find God through taste and touch:

> There is no good trying to be more spiritual than God, God never meant man to be a purely spiritual creature. That is why He uses material things like bread and wine to put the new life into us. We may think this rather crude and unspiritual. God does not: He invented eating. He likes matter. He invented it.[6]

Lewis' point, then, is that the very God who invented eating and matter is a God who permits and encourages us, each in our way, to find God through eating.

At this point, then, let me identify nine ways in which all people can, as it were, "eat the bread of heaven." By *heaven* I mean the Open Space within which the universe unfolds. I mean God. And by the *bread of heaven* I mean God's Breathing, which can indeed be experienced, among other ways, in the eating and sharing of food.

Nine Ways of Knowing God

The first way is *Discernment*. This is an intuitive listening to God's Breathing as an inner teacher or guide. It can be an "act" or a "habit," or both. For example, if a woman is faced with an important decision in her life—whether to change jobs, for example—then "discernment" lies in listening to the deepest promptings within her own heart, trustful that they are of God and from God. This is an act of discernment. If, on the other hand, this woman is having an ordinary day without the need to make major decisions but seems to respond wisely and compassionately to each situation as it arises—laughing when it is time to laugh, being serious when it is time to be serious—then "discernment" lies in her spontaneous and intuitive responsiveness to the call of each moment. This is the habit of discernment. In Christianity, discernment as act and habit is called "following the guidance of the Holy Spirit."

The second is *Sacramental Awareness*. This is awareness of divine presence in people and places, plants and animals, art and music, feelings and events. And, yes, in the eating of food. Sacramental awareness lies in seeing things, feeling things, and touching things with a recognition that they are sacraments through which God is present. It has two forms: delight in beauty and shared intimacy with others.

In both instances God is present as mediated by others, analogous to the way that light shines through a stained glass window. Just as light shines through the various panes of glass, so Holy Light can shine through people and places, plants and animals, art and music, feelings and events. Sacramental Awareness lies in seeing the Light in each vessel of Light. In sharing a meal with another, for example, the sharing and the food itself are vessels through which the Light shines.

The third is *Openness to Healing*. This is inner availability to fresh spiritual energy, which gives energy for life, even when other sources of energy, mental and physical, are depleted. If a man is dying from a debilitating disease, for example, and yet finds the courage to face the disease, he is "receiving fresh energy." When this fresh energy is received in a continuous way, there is a perpetual freshness in each present moment.

The fourth is *Living-by-Dying*. This is a subjective "dropping away" of attachments to personal goals, relationships, systems of belief, and inner needs when they have become "false gods" in our lives. Examples of such false gods are legitimate psychological needs that have become compulsions: a need to be needed, to receive the approval of others, to be in complete control of one's life, to be perfect. When these needs become the central organizing principles of our lives, they need to drop away. This "dropping away" or "letting go" is then followed by a welling up of wisdom, compassion, and freedom. The "letting go" is the dying, and the "welling up" is the living. In the New Testament this process, undergone day by day and moment by moment, is called "death and resurrection."

The fifth is *Trust in Open Space*. This is an interior movement of the soul in which "something goes wide" in our hearts. Another name for this widening is "trust." In this trust we know three things about life. We know (1) that there is a grace sufficient to each moment, (2) that there is a wideness in God's mercy, and (3) that in some mysterious way, all will be well, and all manner of things will be well, even if we do not know how or why. In the New Testament this trust, this widening of the heart and nonverbal knowing, is called "faith." It can be accompanied by different forms of religious belief, and sometimes by no belief at all.

The sixth is *Deep Listening*. Another name for this might be "inner silence." It is relaxed and alert attention to what is happening around us and within us, in a compassionate and nonjudgmental way, without adding additional commentary. It lies in listening to other people on their own terms and for their own sakes without adding one's personal agenda; and it lies in listening to the natural world—to hills and rivers, trees and stars—in a similar spirit. In the Christian tradition this "quiet listening" is another aspect of what is called "the contemplation of nature." It does not involve seeing things as vessels of Holy Light, but rather seeing them as having value in and for themselves. In Buddhism it is called "mindfulness."

The seventh is *Courage in Suffering*. This is facing tragedy with courage, without hiding or running away, even when nothing can be done to "fix" the situation. In some instances this courage involves protest and anger; in other instances it involves a sense of deep peace. In all instances it involves a dim recognition that the suffering is shared by God and enfolded into a deeper and divine love, which does not cause the suffering but rather embraces it.

The eighth is *Creativity*. This is availability to, and actualizing, novel possibilities for healing, wholeness, and beauty in the world. Creativity of this sort includes (1) artistic creativity, such as the creation of poetry, music, and architecture; (2) prophetic creativity, such as the imagining of more just and sustainable ways of living in the world; and (3) domestic creativity, such as the creation of new recipes, new ways of making beds, and new ways of arranging a room so that it looks beautiful. If artistic creativity is exemplified in Mozart; and prophetic creativity is exemplified in Gandhi; then domestic creativity is exemplified by countless unnamed homemakers throughout our world. All forms illustrate availability to divine Breathing.

The ninth is *Loving-kindness.* This is active cooperation with God's Breathing in thought, word, and deed, in which we share in the joys and sufferings of others on their own terms and for their own sakes, and try to promote their happiness. Examples of loving-kindness include taking care of children, baking bread for friends, visiting people in prison, delighting in the happiness of others, appreciating the good qualities of others, and doing daily chores in a good spirit. At best, we enter into loving-kindness without being overly attached to results. We love even if the love seems to bear no fruit. Moreover, we love without needing to be "noticed" by others or "recognized" for our love. In the loving itself, in the sharing in the joy and the suffering of others, there is personal joy.

I suspect that most of us are familiar with most of the nine ways and are particularly gifted in several of them even as we might need to grow in other areas. For example, some people are especially gifted in delight in beauty but need to grow in their capacities for letting go, while others are gifted in creativity but need to grow in their capacities for forgiveness. All nine are important. I think of them as "nine ways to practice the presence" or "nine ways of eating the bread of heaven" or "nine ways of living from the Center."

I would like to make a proposal, and it is twofold: (1) that whenever we enter into these nine ways of experiencing, we are being breathed by God, even if we do not understand the experiences as involving God, and even if we do not believe in God; and (2) that when we enter into these ways, we discover the deepest meaning of our lives. This meaning is not what the advertisements tell us. It is not to "make money" or "be attractive" or "be successful" by marketplace standards. It is to practice the presence of God in our daily lives.

Of course, these nine ways overlap, feed into one another, and reinforce one another. The more "discerning" we are, for example, the more we will exhibit "loving-kindness." And the more "loving" we are, the more able we will be to "listen quietly" to others without adding our own projections. The nine ways are best imagined as nine spokes of a wheel, all leading to and nourished by a center, which is God's Breathing. You can discover God through one spoke and quickly find yourself on another spoke. All this is to the good. God does not simply meet us in one way but rather in many ways, all of which are part of that Way which is itself the Truth and the Life.

Moreover, there may well be more than nine spokes. There may well be eleven, or forty-nine, or three thousand. My list is not exhaustive. This raises an essential question. Given that there may well be so many ways of being available to the Breathing, how can we know if a given experience truly involves availability? How do we know that the qualities at issue—creativity or courage, for example— aren't simply expressions of the vested interests of the ego, or perhaps even subtle conduits for the forces of destruction in the world?

Wisdom, Compassion, and Freedom

Here is my answer. I suggest that a human experience exhibits availability to God's Breathing if it contributes to, or expresses, one or some combination of three qualities: wisdom, compassion, and inner freedom.

Of course, *wisdom* means many things. In the context of this book, wisdom is not a stockpile of information, but rather an outlook on life. It includes an intuitive awareness of the interconnectedness of things; of the impermanence of all things; of the necessary actions in given situations; of the unique value of each living being; and of the embracing of each creature, and the whole of creation, in the embrace of a Great Compassion, a Widened Heart, in God. Thus, "wisdom" includes quiet listening, so that we can sense our connections with things; discernment, in which we are open to fresh possibilities in new situations; and trust in Open Space, through which we sense our enfoldment in the Great Compassion.

Compassion is another word for loving-kindness. It means sharing in the joys and sufferings of living beings, acting to reduce their suffering and promote their well-being. It also includes having compassion for oneself in such a way that one avoids self-inflation and self-deflation. And certainly it includes forgiveness: a capacity to will the well-being of another, even if that person has harmed us. When we have compassion, we "love our neighbors as ourselves," cognizant that our neighbors and ourselves are enfolded in the Great Compassion.

Inner freedom has two meanings. It means freedom *from* hurriedness, distractedness, and inner compulsion, and it means freedom *for* wisdom and compassion in our daily lives. When we enjoy inner freedom, we are free from being inordinately attached to worldly things and from being controlled by inner addictions, and we are free to live openly and honestly, in healing relation to others.

A key sign of this freedom is spontaneity: a capacity to respond to what is happening in the immediacy of the moment in ways that are true to the reality of the situation, and nonclinging. A capacity for hearty laughter, for example, is a sign of spontaneity, as is a capacity for crying. In certain contexts, both laughter and tears are expressions of inner freedom and thus expressions of "availability to the Breathing."

My thesis, then, is this: Whenever we see wisdom, compassion, and inner freedom in a person's life—as expressed in an act of discernment, for example, or in a moment of creativity, or in a moment of quiet listening to a friend in need—we see God's Breathing, thus named or not. In this view, then, there is already a meaningful portion of "availability to the Spirit" in our world. We see "spirituality" in young children and old people, in accountants and plumbers, in grandmothers and homemakers, in sages and clowns. The human heart often is, or can be, a dwelling place, a sanctuary if you will, for God's Breathing. When the heart functions in this way, there is spirituality.

Delight in Beauty and Creativity

Perhaps there is a slight contrast between the view of spirituality that I am developing in this book and the view that you, my reader, have imbibed from other sources. Sometimes the spiritual life is depicted as one that "puts the lid" on human spontaneities or that is overly disciplined. For my part, I think there is a healthy place in the spiritual life for obedience to a disciplined spiritual path: a path of daily prayer and meditation, of worship with others, of participation in sacred communities, of fidelity to a tradition, and of voluntary service to others. We must indeed practice the presence.

Still, there is also a place for wildness. By wildness I do not mean merely random activity or turbulence. I mean something closer to the "wildness" of the artist in her sensitivity to the creativity of the universe, as manifest in the world around us, in her willingness to surrender to this creativity and beauty, to be amazed by it, and then to contribute to it in her own wild way. In terms of the nine forms of spirituality named above, the two that come closest to this wildness are delight in beauty and creativity. Let us conclude by reflecting on them a little more closely.

Consider delight in beauty, itself a form of sacramental awareness. Of course, our world includes much that is horrible and unworthy of delight. It includes rape and murder, selfishness and greed, callousness and cruelty, genocide and infanticide. We must be honest about the world's tragedies. But our world is also filled with much that is immensely beautiful and that calls forth our deepest appreciation: the power of poignant music, the intimacy of a love affair, the excellence of a good idea, the compassion of a grandmother, and, to take a larger perspective, the creativity of a fifteen-billion-year-old cosmos. What, then, is the greatest of these grandeurs? What is the most marvelous of the many wonders we can behold?

In her poem "The Greatest Grandeur," Pattiann Rogers playfully asks these questions and lists some candidates from the cosmos. Her candidates are a delight to the imagination, so I will list them as candidates for your consideration. I am sure that you could add some of your own favorites. Hers include

- the reptilian dance of a purple-tongued sand iguana
- the glow of rust-orange rock in an expansive desert as set against the blue-gray of an approaching rainstorm
- the harmonics of shifting electron rings
- the complex movement of sandpipers crossing each other's paths while flying over a hayfield
- the terror of lightning strikes on prairies, because they make us feel "dwarfed and utterly helpless"
- the cathedral-like waves of stormy seas, because they also make us feel dwarfed and helpless
- the serenity of stars reflected in the calm waters of a placid lake.[7]

In identifying these wonders, Rogers is inviting us not to choose between them, but rather to recognize just how plentiful and varied are the types of beauty in our world. Some are attractive and some frightening, but all are amazing if we have eyes to see. Rogers is playing the role of a biblical psalmist. She is offering a hymn of praise.

However, in her case the praise does not lie in paying metaphysical compliments to God, important as that might be. Rather, it lies in being appreciative of, and humbled by, a beautiful planet of bone and flesh, color and sound, mystery and grace. In this appreciation and humility, I suggest, there is God's Breathing.

To be sure, God's Breathing is also objective and independent of human existence. It is a breath of life within the iguanas and sandpipers, quite apart from their perception by human beings. It is their inner animating principle and their lure toward satisfactory survival. Still, this animating principle is not only within them, but also within us: in our capacity to let go of our preconceptions and human-centeredness and simply be awed by their beauty. Whenever we delight in beauty, we are being animated by God's Breathing, even if we do not believe in a God who breathes.

This points to one conviction of this book, that spirituality cannot be reduced to "believing the right things" or even "doing the right things." A healthy life has three dimensions: intellectual understanding, practical action, and spiritual depth. Each of these dimensions is important, and each can nourish the other. But none is reducible to the other. We can be intellectually developed, for example, but nevertheless lack spiritual depth and practical skills. The ideal is to have the three in balance. It is to be a whole person: mind, body, and spirit.

The third dimension, spiritual depth, pertains to the subjective capacities for wisdom, compassion, and inner freedom. For example, delight in beauty is a form of wisdom. It lies in feeling the presence of things around us, and within us, in a way that is honest about, and thus amazed by, their integrity and beauty. In this amazement there is an intuitive wisdom that cannot be reduced to intellectual understanding. It is a knowing that occurs through feeling rather than thinking. Often we see this knowing in children, who are so easily amazed by what they see, even as they lack concepts to name what they are seeing. In their amazement there is a divine wisdom. As adults our aim should not be to return to childhood, but to become as little children, at least as is witnessed in their capacities for amazement. It is to learn to see the world freshly and freely, as if for the first time. In this amazement—in this capacity for wonder—there is spiritual depth.

Consider now another form of spiritual wildness: creativity. Rogers concludes her poem with the suggestion that the greatest grandeur does not lie in the world around us but in the pure potentiality—the dark emptiness—of every next moment.

> But it is the dark emptiness contained
> in every next moment that seems to me
> the most singularly glorious gift,
> that void which one is free to fill
> with processions of men bearing burning
> cedar knots or with parades of blue horses,[8]

Here, too, she points to God's Breathing. There is indeed something amazing, something quite beautiful, in the fact that each present moment of our lives is open to a "next moment" that we can fill with new events, real and imagined. From this freedom we create concrete objects that serve the world, including

with hammered silver teapots or kiln-dried
crockery, tangerine and almond custards,
polonaises, polkas, whittling sticks, wailing
walls; that space large enough to hold all
invented blasphemies and pieties, 10,000
definitions of god and more, never fully
filled, never.[9]

Equally important, it is from the freedom of this moment that we can create healing bonds with other people, even when relationships have been strained in the past. We can choose to forgive and to ask forgiveness, to love and to receive love, to share and to listen. Compassion and empathy, no less than teapots and custard, are the results of deep creativity. Whenever we open ourselves to the next moment, whenever we trust in fresh possibilities for healing and wholeness, we are being available to the mystery at the heart of creation. We are living from the Center.

Earlier I said that this deeper Center has many names. It can be called the *Spirit of God* or the *Holy Spirit* or the *Breath of Life* or *Divine Energy* or *God's Breathing.* It is from our sensitivity to this Breathing, conscious and unconscious, that we come up with our 10,000 definitions of God and God's Breathing, none adequate but many helpful.

Even as we arrive at such definitions, it is important to remember that God is always more than our definitions and that God's Breathing is more than our names. This Center is more than an idea. It is a healing and creative spirit that has inspired the universe to produce iguanas, cooks to create custards, theologians to create definitions of God, and grandmothers to become saints. Spirituality does not lie in our belief in this spirit. Rather, it lies in our openness to this Spirit, day by day and moment by moment, in ways that are wise, compassionate, and free.

CHAPTER TWO

This Wild and Precious Life
Spirituality as Sacramental Awareness

> *The miracle is not to walk on water.*
> *The miracle is to walk on the green earth*
> *In the present moment.*
>
> Thich Nhat Hanh[1]

> *Tell me, what is it you plan to do*
> *With your one wild and precious life?*
>
> Mary Oliver[2]

> *Do not store up for yourselves treasures on earth...You*
> *cannot serve God and wealth...And why do you worry*
> *about clothing?*
>
> Matthew 6:19, 24, 28

Imagine, if you will, that you are taking a walk on a cool summer morning. It is Sunday and perhaps some of your friends are at church, but on this morning your sanctuary is a grassy field, and your worship is the slow pace of walking. In keeping with the mood of the morning, you kneel in the grass and reflect on nature's many miracles. You think about the gracefulness of the swan, the power of the black bear, and the strange beauty of the grasshopper.

You think about the grasshopper because, in the immediacy of the moment, you are holding one in the palm of your hand. She is eating a lump of sugar that you brought with you. You are humbled and awed by your newfound friend: her enormous and complicated eyes, her jaws that move back and forth rather than up and down, her pale green forearms, her ability to wash her face and then, when she is finished, to fly away in a direction of her choosing. Each grasshopper is unique, you think to yourself. Each one has its wild and precious life.

And you, too, have such a life. What will you do with it in the months and years to come? Indeed, what will you do with it for the remainder of this day?

Slowly an insight emerges within you, not exactly from your conscious mind, but from a deeper place, like a gut feeling. *I don't know exactly what prayer is,* you say to yourself, *but I do know how to pay attention, how to kneel in the grass, how to be idle and blessed, how to stroll through the fields.* You realize that your gift for paying attention is your way of praying, your way of communing with the rest of creation. You decide you will extend your prayer into the afternoon. You walk through the woods until dusk.

As it becomes dark and you turn toward home, a familiar yet hostile voice enters your mind. *What have you been doing all afternoon? Why haven't you been productive? What have you accomplished? You've been wasting your time.*

You distrust this voice. You have heard it often enough at work and even from some of your closest friends. Still, it does not represent your core values. Behind the voice is a way of thinking that suggests that the very purpose of life is to be productive and accomplish things, to be acquisitive and successful, to stay busy and make money. It says that grasshoppers and bears and swans aren't really very important, at least as compared to prestige and wealth and achievement. It says that paying attention, that praying, is really a waste of time.

This is not what you believe. You have nothing against hard work; you've been working hard all your life. But you believe that hard work ought to be punctuated by periods of sabbath, of rest, of refreshment. And you believe that the true purpose of life is not just to have things, but to become who God created you to be. It is to live wisely and compassionately in the world, moved by its beauty and sensitive to its sufferings. The hostile voice forgets this love. It thinks that "being busy" is the purpose of life.

In a moment of inner boldness, then, you speak back to the voice. Here, too, your words come from the deeper place. *Tell me, what else should I have done?* you say to the voice. *Doesn't everything die at last, and too soon? Tell me, what is it you plan to do with your one wild and precious life?* And with this utterance, at least for a moment, the voice disappears. What is left is the silence and the brilliance of your own life.

Inner Wisdom and Outer Sacraments

I borrow and use this image of an attentive walker, trustful of grasshoppers and distrustful of hostile voices, from a poem by Mary Oliver called "The Summer Day."[3] I have embellished her image to suit my purposes, but many of the words come from her poem, and I refer to this woman stroller and her experiences throughout this chapter.

Most of us, I suspect, are like the stroller. We work hard; we need to balance hard work with times of rest; and we want to live attentively and lovingly in the world. We want to make the best of our wild and precious lives. How can we do this?

I think we do this, not by willfully engineering our lives into success as defined by consumer culture, but by willingly surrendering to a Mystery deep within the heart of creation and our own lives. My name for this Mystery is God. And my name for its presence in our lives is God's Breathing.

By God I mean a sky-like Mind within which the universe lives and moves and has its being. We might compare God to a cosmic Womb within which the universe has been unfolding, epoch by epoch, moment by moment, throughout its fifteen-billion-year history. Or to an opened Heart within whose mysterious embrace all beings dwell: the stars and planets, the hills and rivers, the trees and stars, the people and grasshoppers.

Given these analogies, God's Breathing would then be the amniotic fluid—the baptismal waters—of this cosmic Womb, as these waters flow into the lives of the various creatures, giving them energy for life. Or the gentle breathing of the opened Heart, as its freshness is inhaled by every creature, each in its own unique way. However we might imagine this Breathing, the point is clear: Our need is to be open to the Breathing in our daily lives, each in our own way.

Gut feelings represent one form of availability to the Breathing. The Breathing can be present in our lives as an Inner Guide, an inner Wisdom, by which we feel inwardly lured toward healing and wholeness relative to the situation at hand. We are aware of this lure through deeply felt intuitions and promptings. In the case of our stroller, for example, these were promptings for saying yes to the prospect of walking in the woods and paying attention to grasshoppers and no to the prospect of feeling guilty about it.

From the perspective of process theology, the promptings of this inner Wisdom consist of two realities at once: (1) fresh possibilities for wisdom, compassion, and inner freedom relative to the immediate circumstances of our lives; and (2) an inner desire to actualize these possibilities, to make them real in our lives. The fresh possibilities are God's will for the moment, and the inner desire is God's prayer within us. Together God's will and God's prayer form one feeling, one prompting, which Christians call guidance from the Holy Spirit. Our task is to listen to the ongoing prayer of God within our own hearts. In Christianity this listening, this openness, is called "discernment."

Holy Communion

The grasshopper in the poem represents still another way that God's Breathing can be at work in our lives. Here the Breathing is not an inner guide but rather an outer presence or, more precisely, a healing energy that flows through an outer presence. The outer presence is a sacrament or holy icon, and the healing energy is God's Breathing. Our reception of this energy is sacramental awareness.

Of course, for most of us, our most cherished sacraments on a daily basis are other human beings. These icons include the people we love: our friends, family, neighbors, strangers, and even people who have harmed us or whom we have harmed. Our sacramental awareness takes the form of friendship, love, affection, confession, and forgiveness; of shared laughter, shared suffering, shared intimacy, and shared destinies. In all these relationships the prayer of God is being realized.

Moreover, it is being realized in community. The teaching of Christianity and other religions is that God becomes incarnate in the world, not simply within individuals in the privacy of their hearts, but also *between* individuals in their relations with each other, particularly when those relations are mutually enhancing. When people enjoy community with one another, when they share one another's feelings and care about one another, the will of God is done on earth as it is in heaven. People are enjoying *holy communion.*

Of course, as our stroller well recognized, other living beings, too, can be sacraments. They, too, are part of that church—that sacred community—to which we belong. As Thomas Berry puts it, the universe itself is a communion of subjects, not a collection of objects.

Accordingly, we often find God in communion with the rest of creation: the other ninety-nine percent. Witness the healing that so many us find in relations with dogs, cats, horses, and other companion animals. Witness also the peace that so many people feel in the presence of green plants, in the beauty of wild animals, in the contours of landscapes, and in the glimmering of stars and galaxies. When it comes to God-breathed presences, we are not limited to other humans.

In some instances, the communion we feel with the rest of creation may indeed be a kind of intimacy as described above. I myself have two dogs with whom I share psychic space, such that we feel one another's feelings and share in one another's destinies. Admittedly, I do not always know what they are thinking, and they do not always know what I am thinking. Sometimes we are strangers to one another. Still, I know them well enough to know when they are lonely, bored, angry, and happy. And they know me well too. We enjoy deep human-animal bonds, to the mutual enhancement of all of us. Along with my family, they are part of my local church.

In other instances, our communion will not involve such intimacy, but will nevertheless involve a subtler sense of communion, of kinship, with the rest of creation, combined with a deep respect for otherness. This is what our stroller felt as she gazed into the eyes of the grasshopper. Let us call this *delight in beauty.*

Clearly, delight in beauty can often be enjoyed in communion with the natural world, but it can also be enjoyed in relation to human creations. Art, music, architecture, and poetry can be channels of grace in our lives. And it is possible that certain human inventions—the microscope and the telescope, the pencil and the computer—can likewise be channels. Some people meet God quite intimately in such creations, perhaps especially in music. I know a man—a jazz musician—who believes in God, not because he has been convinced of God philosophically, but because he hears something divine and beautiful in the melodies and rhythms of music. For him the word of God is not first of all a book or even a messiah from Nazareth, but rather the sound—the living vibration—of beautiful music. In the sound itself, he finds God. Oftentimes, when I listen to him play, I hear God too.

Finally, before leaving sacramental awareness, let us note that even tragic experiences and personal pain can be sacraments. They are not sacraments because they are willed or even permitted by God. God does not exactly shine through the eyes of a torturer with the beauty, say, that God shines through the eyes of a grasshopper on a summer day. From the perspective of this book, there are some things that happen in life that even God cannot prevent. Still, there is nothing that can happen that cannot itself be made into a sacrament if we face it with courage, grow from it, and transmute its horror into love. Tragic happenings can make us very bitter or very loving. When they make us loving, and when they lead us to want to help make the world a better place, they have become sacraments.

The Ten Temptations of Consumerism

The hostile voice in the story of our stroller represents another reality in our lives. It is not a fresh possibility from the inner teacher or the healing energy of a holy sacrament, but rather what Christianity calls a "temptation." It is an inner urge that, if followed, leads us into greed, hatred, and confusion.

A negative urge such as this can arise from a variety of sources. It can come from a broken heart, a confused mind, a malevolent will, or a corrupting cultural atmosphere. In our story, the negative urge is of the latter sort. It comes from the cultural atmosphere of consumerism. Here the temptation is a call toward compulsive busyness, but it could as easily have been a call toward compulsive greed, envy, or acquisitiveness. Such is the nature of consumer culture. It is a voice with many calls.

Consider the following calls of consumer culture. I call them the Ten Temptations of Consumerism. They are to believe

- That appearance, affluence, and achievement are—and ought to be—the central organizing principles of our lives
- That being compulsively busy, even to the point of exhaustion, is a sign of healthy and productive living
- That having a successful career is more important than being a good parent, being a good neighbor, being a kind and loving person, or taking walks in the woods
- That good work is reducible to making money, and that unpaid work—particularly in the home—is not really working
- That the appropriate goal of life—higher than service to the poor or service to God—is to enjoy prosperity in the suburbs with the perfectly manicured lawn
- That depression can be cured by shopping
- That the most important thing in life is to "have my needs met"
- That we humans are not citizens of our communities, much less vessels of God's love, but rather "consumers" who participate in a "global marketplace," and that other creatures are "commodities" for our use

- That the universe is not a communion of subjects, but rather a collection of objects
- That we are all on our own, because there is no grace—no ultimate mercy—within the depths of things

If you hear these voices within your own mind, as I often do, I hope that you might recognize them, not as examples of divine prayer within you, but rather as enemies of your better self. They are examples of what the Bible calls "temptations."

What, then, is the alternative to these temptations? What are, as it were, the Ten Healing Alternatives? I think they are to know

- That living lightly on the Earth and gently with each other is much more important than appearance, affluence, and achievement
- That healthy living requires not only creativity, action, and good work but also rest and relaxation, so that our work can be productive rather than compulsive
- That it is much more important to be a good parent, be a good neighbor, and be a good person than to have a successful career, particularly if "success" is defined purely in monetary terms
- That truly good work does not consist in making money or in exploiting natural resources, but rather in serving others, often without being noticed
- That helping others, and dwelling in solidarity with people in need, is more important than prosperity in the suburbs
- That compulsive shopping is a symptom of disease, not a cure for depression
- That the world is not a global marketplace, but rather a gorgeous planet, filled with many creatures, each of whom is loved by God on its own terms and for its own sake, and each of whom contains God within.
- That happiness lies not necessarily in "having my needs met," but rather in living simply and in service to others
- That the universe is a communion of subjects, not a collection of objects
- That we are not on our own, because the universe is enfolded within an ultimate grace that renders questions of "success" and "failure" irrelevant

I think these ten alternatives approximate the kind of outlook our stroller sought as she spoke back to the hostile voices. They are the kind of outlook I wish to recommend as well. They represent some of the values that derive from a life lived spiritually in the age of consumerism.

Spirituality as Openness to God's Breathing

By spirituality I do not mean a mystical state of consciousness to be enjoyed in moments of ecstasy, although such moments have their place in life. All of us need times when we lose our sense of individual identity and feel at one with the universe, with life, with God. In consumer society we seek such ecstasy in various ways: alcohol, sex, meditation, sports, music, prayer, movies, and the stock market. Some are healthy and some are not, but all reveal a natural need for heightened states of consciousness.

Nevertheless, by spirituality I mean something more daily and ordinary, which can include moments of ecstasy but which can also include moments of boredom, anxiety, tension, and depression. I mean openness to God's Breathing, day by day and moment by moment, in ways that are wise, compassionate, and inwardly free. In this view, spirituality can be enjoyed at home and in the workplace, while alone and with others, in darkness and in light, amid sound and silence. We live spiritually when we delight in the good things in life without clinging to them when they pass away. And we live spiritually when we share in the sufferings of others without hiding or running away. Spirituality is ordinary life itself, obedient to the call of the moment, and lived from a deeper Center.

For many of us, the desire to live from the Center begins with a simple desire to be happy. We hear within our own lives a prayer that says, "There is a better way to live, a happier way, a way that is more wise, compassionate, and free. There is a better way to make the best of our wild and precious lives."

Oftentimes, though, it is difficult to quiet down sufficiently to hear this prayer. Our stroller faced this problem; hence her need to take a walk in the woods. I face it too. Thus, I cannot offer you a quick fix to the problem of a chatterbox mind. There are some practical steps that I think we might take, each in our own way, to be more discerning of God's call in our lives. I will go into these in detail in chapter 4, but in brief they are: (1) learning to be silent; (2) becoming mindful of the temptations of consumerism; (3) noticing ways in which God has already been breathing in our lives, even apart from our knowing it;

and (4) actively cooperating with God's Breathing through service to others, lifestyle simplification, prayer, and meditation. I think these steps can help.

But here I would simply like to recommend some guidelines for discernment that might help us in a general way to become more attentive to the divine call within each of us. They come from process theology and represent what might be called a "process approach" to discernment.

Five Guidelines for Discernment

The first guideline is to keep in mind that the fresh possibility we receive from God in a given situation is rarely clear and distinct, but usually vague and dim. To be sure, our capacities for discernment can be enriched by reason and analysis, calculation and logic. They can also be enriched by paying attention to the world around us; that is, by gazing into the eyes of grasshoppers. But ultimately, the objects of discernment—the fresh possibilities themselves—are not concepts or numbers that we entertain with our minds, or even forearms and eyeballs that we see with our eyes. Rather, they are inner urges, like gut feelings. These inner lures do not have clearly marked boundaries that we can master with our minds. They are objects of intuition rather than objects of intellection. If we are to hear God's voice in our lives, it helps if we have a tolerance for vagueness. As Whitehead somewhere put it: "The most important things are vague. An overriding concern with clarity is the bane of little minds."

This respect for vagueness—for insights that are dim but important—has implications for those of us who seek personal guidance from sacred texts such as the Bible. If we are looking for guidance concerning what we might do in a given situation, we can turn to the time-tested teachings of sacred texts. In many instances they are records of discernment, repositories of various ways in which people have listened to, and responded to, Divine Wisdom. Moreover, sacred texts can be sacraments in their own right: finite vessels through which divine presence shines. There is much wisdom to be discerned in the teachings of Jesus and the lessons of Moses, in the insight of the Buddha and the music of the Koran. So often they represent what Huston Smith calls "the distilled wisdom of the human race."[4]

But we must always remember (1) that these teachings are fallible and finite, because they are combined with the cultural limitations and prejudices of their human authors, and (2) that even as these teachings may provide verbalized wisdom, they are but verbal

expressions of deeper intuitions that originally came to their authors—
the authors of the New Testament, for example, or the Dhammapada—
through preverbal lures for feeling. Accordingly, the words and letters
need not be absolutized; it is the wisdom behind the words, which
gave rise to the words, that is more important. When we learn from
sacred texts, we do not learn from the words themselves but from the
experiences that gave rise to the words. Most importantly, we must
learn to find these experiences within ourselves.

The second guideline is to recognize that the fresh possibilities
for healing and wholeness can work within us at various levels:
emotional, intellectual, or bodily. God's prayer can be a fresh possibility
(1) for feeling in a way that integrates old feelings into new patterns
and that helps heal us of unresolved issues from the past; (2) for
understanding ourselves and the world in a new way, moving past
habitual ways of thinking that enslave us in limited visions of ourselves
and reality; and (3) for moving our arms and legs; that is, for walking
or sitting still. In the case of our stroller, for example, the fresh possibility
within her included an unmistakably bodily component. God's prayer
was not simply that she think and feel in new ways. It was also that
she keep walking. Her response to this prayer included a bodily act.
She responded to the spirit, not only with her mind and heart, but
also with her feet. Sometimes this is our calling too. It is not only to
think and feel, it is to do.

The third guideline, which follows from the second, is to be mindful
of the fact that the Divine Wisdom to which we are open in
discernment is not itself an exclusively divine wisdom but also, as it
were, a natural wisdom. By natural wisdom I mean a wisdom that is
found within hills and rivers, trees and stars, molecules and atoms,
living cells and living bodies. It is the Wisdom of God as found in the
wisdom of the Earth and heavens.

As with human wisdom, this natural wisdom is not absolute. A
cancer cell may seek the fullness of unlimited growth, but the wisdom
of the cancer cell is incompatible with the wisdom of the body.
Nevertheless, our very bodies are often discerning of what they need,
even when our minds are unaware of these needs. The point, then, is
that if we are to be discerning of what God calls us toward, it can help
if we listen to the wisdom of our bodies and the wisdom of the natural
world around us. It can help if we pay attention to grasshoppers and
to our own breathing. So often they become sacraments through which
we find fresh possibilities from the healing spirit of God.

The fourth guideline is to remember that the fresh possibilities we receive from God can work in us unconsciously as well as consciously, which is to say that we can receive guidance from the Holy Spirit in our dreams and visions no less than in our ordinary waking consciousness, and also that our responses to these fresh possibilities can be unconscious as well as conscious. On the one hand, this means that we can indeed pay attention to dreams, personal and cosmic, as means through which God is speaking to us and in us. For my part, I know people whose dreams speak to them in quite profound ways, and I know people who have had intense visionary experiences in various kinds of meditation. I trust that God speaks to these people through these experiences, just as God speaks to people through art and music, friendships and silence. On the other hand, it means that even if we do not pay attention to our dreams, they may nevertheless play a role in our lives, as can our unconscious responses to them. We can wake up one morning and realize, to our surprise, that we have grown a little more wise and compassionate, a little less compulsive and more free, even as we cannot consciously remember a single step we took in this direction. We have been responding to God unconsciously, even as we have not been aware of that influence consciously. We have been unconsciously discerning.

Fifth, and finally, it is important to note that the fresh possibility for healing and wholeness that we receive from God in a given situation can also be received by others, in a different way, such that we are called into occasions of communal discernment where we jointly respond to a commonly held dream. For example, the woman in our story felt called into a way of living to which many others in our age simultaneously feel called. The fresh possibility that she felt is one that, perhaps, we too feel; namely, a possibility for living past the greed, envy, and confusion of consumer culture. Different people can feel the same possibility from different points of view, such that, as biblical authors put it, God acts in collective history and not simply in individual humans. Discernment can be a group process as well as an individual process. In our time, there is a profound need for such communal discernment.

Toward what, then, are we communally called in our age of consumerism? Perhaps the ten healing alternatives named above come close to our collective calling. We are called to become people who live lightly on the Earth and gently with each other, respectful of life in all its diversity. It is because consumer society seems so antagonistic to this hope that we find ourselves so critical of consumerism. Our very resistance to consumerism, our willingness to say no to it, is itself an act of discernment. In what follows, then, I want to say more about what I mean by consumerism.

The Lifestyle of Consumerism

By consumerism I do not mean the consuming of material goods and services. All of us need food, clothing, and shelter. Most of us want to enjoy some of the simple and beautiful things in life: good furniture, comfortable clothing, enjoyable food, and beautiful music. One of the problems with a consumer society is that it is not materialistic enough. If we loved matter more, we wouldn't use it so wastefully. We would take care of old things—like old furniture, old clothes, old shoes, and old homes—and love them.

In our time the very act of loving old things, of preserving old homes, old clothes, and old neighborhoods, and also old fields and old forests, is a radical and countercultural act. But actually it is a mode of sacramental awareness, a way of being available to the Breathing. If this is what we mean by "materialism," then this book is an unabashed celebration of materialism.

By consumerism, I mean something very different. I mean (1) an overconsuming lifestyle, characteristic of about one-fifth of the world's population, which is beyond the carrying capacity of the planet, and (2) a set of values and attitudes, promulgated twenty-four hours a day on radio and television, that celebrate and reinforce this overconsuming lifestyle, which we are taught to call "the good life."

We practitioners of consumerism are a minority, but we are now spread throughout the world. We live in North America, Western Europe, Japan, Australia, Hong Kong, and Singapore; and among the affluent classes of Eastern Europe, Latin America, South Africa, and South Korea. Many of us drive privately owned automobiles, eat prepackaged foods, depend on throwaway goods, drink from aluminum cans, enjoy temperature-controlled climates, thrive on a meat-based diet, fly in airplanes, and release inordinate amounts of waste into the atmosphere. As explained in the Introduction, we consume approximately 40 percent of the world's fresh water, 60 percent of its fertilizers, 75 percent of its energy, 75 percent of its timber, 80 percent of its paper, 85 percent of its aluminum. Our aerosol cans, air conditioners, and factories release almost 90 percent of the chlorofluorocarbons that cause ozone depletion. Our use of fossil fuels causes two-thirds of the emissions of carbon dioxide. If the whole world consumed as we consume and polluted as we pollute, the life-support systems of our planet would quickly collapse.

Many of us say that we are "struggling to make ends meet," and indeed we are, though not because we lack food to eat or the basic necessities of life. We spend much of our time struggling to maintain a way of living that we are taught to call the good life, but that often seems breathless and frantic. Caught between the needs of job and family, of personal desire and civic responsibility, we fall into a compulsive busyness, always on our way toward a happiness that never quite arrives. We yearn for a simpler life, one that is more spiritual and caring.

Even as we are "struggling to make ends meet," however, we need to be mindful of the way the rest of the world lives. The other four-fifths of our human family are divided into two groups: the sustainers and the destitute.

The sustainers form about three-fifths of the world's population and live mostly in Latin America, the Middle East, China, and among the non-affluent areas in East Asia. Typically they earn between $700 and $7500 a year per family member, eat more grains than meats, drink clean water, ride bicycles and buses, and depend more on durable goods than throwaways.[5] They are sustainers because they live at levels that could be "sustained" into the indefinite future if global population were to be stabilized and clean technologies employed.

The destitute are the abjectly poor of the world. They are about one-fifth of the world's population and live mostly in rural Africa and rural India. They earn less than $700 a year per family member, eat insufficient grain, drink unclean water, and travel by walking.[6] Their lives are in no way "sustainable." Their deepest need is to rise to the level of the sustainer class.

What, then, is the best hope for our planet? It is (1) that the population of the world cease growing, (2) that nations begin to rely on clean technologies to feed and furnish their citizens, (3) that the truly poor of the world rise from their poverty with some combination of external assistance and local self-development, and (4) that the overconsumers learn to live more simply. In short, it is that the overconsumers and underconsumers meet in the middle, where the sustainers live.

In our time this hope is part of "the great work." God's Breathing is an inwardly felt call within each of us, not only to become whole as individuals but also to be healers in a broken world. Practically speaking, this means to have fewer children, to help create environmentally benign technologies, to serve the poor, and, if we are overconsumers, to live more simply. For many of us, then, the great work will also be hard work. As any addict knows, it can be hard to "let go" of a lifestyle that is hazardous to one's health.

As noted above, however, consumerism is not simply an overconsuming lifestyle. It is also, and perhaps even more perniciously, a set of attitudes and values that celebrate and reinforce the lifestyle, calling it "the good life." These attitudes and values feed the addiction.

The Theology of Consumerism

For pedagogical purposes, it can help if we understand these attitudes and values as an unofficial but corporate-sponsored world religion.

Of course, consumerism is not a religious tradition in the sense that Roman Catholicism is a religious tradition. It does not have a Vatican or a pope or a single text, such as the Bible, to which it appeals for authority. Rather, it is a religion in the sense that Confucianism is a religion. Just as Confucianism is a set of attitudes and values that once shaped so many East Asian cultures, so consumerism is a set of attitudes and values that now shape all cultures. The attitudes of Confucianism include an emphasis on the primacy of the family, the importance of respecting elders, and the value of tradition. Analogously, the attitudes of consumerism include an emphasis on the primacy of the individual, the importance of staying young, and the value of newness. Both religions give people a sense of what life is about. In what follows I want to say a word about the history of consumerism as a religion and then caricature its theology.

Many world religions begin as sects. Christianity began as a sect in the Middle East, Islam as a sect in the Arabian Peninsula, and Buddhism as a sect in India. Large social movements have small beginnings. If consumerism is now a world religion, or at least a quasi-religion, then it, too, began as a sect. Its geographical origin was the United States.

In *Land of Desire: Merchants, Power, and the Rise of a New American Culture,* William Leach traces the early development of this religion.[7] He shows how, beginning in 1890, America was transformed into a nation of consumers through the concerted efforts of retail giants such as Marshall Field and John Wanamaker. Their need was to create an ever-growing demand for the goods they offered for sale. With an unprecedented use of window displays and advertising, and also with the support of government, education, and even church, they convinced people of four things: (1) that happiness is to be found through the acquisition and consumption of material goods, (2) that it is better to have "new" goods than old ones, (3) that everyone, not just the affluent elite, can enjoy the fruits of consumption-driven desire, and (4) that money is the primary measure of value in society.

According to Leach, these four attitudes gradually came to shape the whole of American society, despite dissenting voices among Christians and others. Within the span of half a century, Americans became a nation of consumers, lured by the promise of "comfort and bodily well-being...with more goods this year than last, and more next year than this."[8] This promise of comfort and acquisition became what many Americans now call "the American dream." So powerful is this dream today that any criticism of it is often considered blasphemous.

For many of us, "the American Dream" seems so natural that we take it as "the human dream." It does indeed have tremendous mythic power, tapping into some of our most fundamental needs for pleasure and adventure. It is important to recognize, however, that it was a new dream in many ways, and it differed from earlier American dreams. It differed from the way of the Puritans, for example, who emphasized frugality and thrift, hard work and community living, moderation and devotion to spiritual concerns. It differed also from the way of the Quakers, many of whom found life's deepest meanings in simplicity and tolerance, not ever-increasing consumption. And it differed from the way of the original Americans, the Native Americans, for whom living within the limits of the land, and in obedience to the way of the elders, was so often a necessity.

This is not to say that the Puritans, Quakers, and Native Americans avoided consumption. Like all of us, they consumed material goods. Nor is it to say that consumerism had no roots in still earlier dreams of Western peoples. To the contrary, consumerism's emphasis on newness can rightly be understood as a questionable development of the biblical theme that God comes to us, not only from the past and present, but also from the future. Let me explain.

In Hebrew Scripture and in the New Testament, we find the idea that God appears to humans in the form of fresh possibilities for a messianic age, an age of peace and justice, a coming kingdom, a new Jerusalem. Jews and Christians alike look forward to a time when "the will of God will be done on Earth as it is in heaven." In some ways consumerism, with its dream of endless material progress, is an expression of this forward-looking hope. The difference, however, is that in consumerism, the hoped-for future is understood in purely material terms. From the vantage point of consumerism, the will of God will be done on Earth as it is in heaven, not when wisdom and compassion reign in our hearts, but rather when corporations rule the world, when there is perfect competition between workers for corporate-sponsored jobs, and when the world is united as a global consumer culture. Then, so it seems, the new age will truly have arrived. Then people can enjoy what life is truly about: endless material prosperity. The difference between the American dream of the Quakers, Puritans, and Native Americans and the American dream of the consumer society is that the former positioned material prosperity within the larger horizons of more spiritual forms of existence, whereas the latter takes "endless material prosperity" as the central organizing principle of life.

What has happened, of course, is that now this new American dream has been exported to the whole of the world through corporate advertising and mass media. Today many societies, and not just American society, have come to organize their lives around the hope that they can live like the Americans, enjoying more goods next year than this year, and never having to say, "Enough." The new American dream has become a world dream. Indeed, as I suggest, it has become a religion. Let me offer an unflattering caricature of its theology.

Its central organizing principle—and thus its god—is economic growth for its own sake. This does not mean that the followers of consumerism worship growth as a personal god. Many of us are Christian or Buddhist or Jewish or Muslim. At night when we go to bed, we do not say "Dear Economic Growth." Rather we say "O Heavenly Father" or "O Holy Spirit" or "Mother of Creation."

Still, we worship "growth" as a principle around which we organize our collective energies, trustful that it brings untold benefits to life. We elect politicians who promise us "growth" and oust those who fail to deliver it, and we judge our own collective well-being on whether or not we are "growing."

If Growth is the god, then the priests of consumerism are the politicians, economists, and corporate executives who understand the mysteries of growth and can help us gain access to it; the evangelists are the advertisers who display for us the products of such growth and convince us that we cannot be happy without them; the laity are those of us who are influenced by these advertisements and then buy the products of growth; and the church is the mall.

Religious education occurs when we are children and our parents take us to this church. Or perhaps a little later, when we cruise the mall with our friends. We see the window displays—the consumerist version of stained glass windows—and we want to buy the products inside them. We realize that we need money in order to buy them, and thus we begin to think that money is the most important thing in life. The acquisition of money then becomes our primary ritual.

The salvation offered by consumerism comes through appearance, affluence, and marketable achievement. We feel saved, or made whole, when we appear (or think we appear) to be successful and attractive to others, when we feel good about how much money we have (which always has to be as much as, or more than, others), and when we can take pride in accomplishments that make sense in the marketplace. The "saints" of consumerism are, then, the people who are "fully saved" by these standards. They are the "successful" executives of very large corporations and the celebrities who "have it all" and who show us what it is like to have it all.

Like other religions, consumerism also has its creeds and doctrines. The creeds include the ideas that Bigger Is Better, Faster Is Better, More Is Better, and You Can Have It All. The "doctrine of creation" is that the Earth is real estate to be bought and sold in the marketplace. And the "doctrine of human existence" is that we humans are skin-encapsulated egos, cut off from the world by the boundaries of our skin, whose highest good lies in "having our needs met." A corollary of the latter idea is that the very purpose of the surrounding world is to "meet my needs." An advertising jingle for Budweiser beer puts it well when it says, "This Bud's for You." Except that consumerism adds, "And the whole world is for you too."

The Budweiser Christian

Obviously, these teachings contradict the core principles of almost all the other world religions. Consider a more prayerful Christianity. It tells us that Small Is Beautiful, Good Things Come Slowly, Enough Is Enough, and We Don't Even Need It All. It says that our purpose in life is not to be attractive, wealthy, or even productive, but rather to love. It reminds us that we find ourselves not when we live for private satisfactions, but when we lose ourselves. It offers the shocking claim that the universe does not really belong to us, but rather the other way around: We belong to the universe, and still more deeply to the God who encompasses it.

The problem, of course, is that this prayerful approach to life is drowned out by the louder voice of consumerism. Or worse, absorbed into it. Many Christians now believe that appearance, affluence, and achievement are signs of being blessed by God; that bigger churches are inevitably better; that the good news can be marketed like a commodity; and that this universe, or at least this earth, is indeed "for us." We have become Budweiser Christians.

In this book, then, I hope to present a theological and spiritual alternative to "the good life" as conceived by consumerism. It is the abundant life of which Jesus speaks in the gospel of John. This is the life we live when we "receive the Spirit" and thus "live from the Breathing." This abundant life is not limited to Christians. People of other religions and of no religion can receive the Spirit and live from it. They can cooperate with God's grace and live from the Center, even if they do not name this Center "God."

Still, one thing that is necessary for abundant living is freedom from self-preoccupation and self-aggrandizement. Most people who know "abundant living" and who "live from the Center" are neither famous nor wealthy nor powerful. They are ordinary people: grandmothers and grandfathers, auto mechanics and clerks, farmers and grocers, children and small business people. They do not center their lives around having "my needs met." Rather, they have surrendered to a higher power, a deeper self, a wider context, a sacred whole: God's Breathing. If there is value in this book, I hope that it helps you and me alike live less consumptively and more abundantly.

The desire to live more abundantly is itself part of God's prayer within each human heart. At its most basic level, it is a desire for happiness, for ourselves and ultimately for all living beings. This desire belongs both to God and to us. Not only are we co-creators with God, we are also co-desirers, co-prayers. No less than God, our own deepest prayer is that the will of God be done "on Earth as it is in heaven."

Jesus at the Mall

In order to do the will of God on Earth as it is in heaven, we must go against the will of consumerism. And this is no easy feat, because consumerism is not easy to fight. To the contrary, one reason that consumerism is so successful is that it is very tolerant. In order to join its ranks, you are not required to relinquish your old religion. You can be converted to consumerism and yet, in the privacy of your heart, still believe that you worship God through Christ, or Allah through the Koran, or that you seek enlightenment in the way of the Buddha, or understanding through science. All that consumerism requires is (1) that you consume, burn up, wear out, and discard material goods at ever-increasing rates; (2) that you learn to look at others in terms of appearance, affluence, and marketable achievement; and (3) that you ignore those teachings of your personal religion that recommend a simpler lifestyle and a less materialistic set of values. If we are Christian, for example, then all that consumerism requires is that we break the heart of Jesus.

Imagine Jesus looking down from his cross during Christmas season. Gazing into a mall, he remembers having cautioned his followers about the worship of money and having counseled them not to worry about material possessions. He remembers having said that, just as the lilies can live simply in their God-given beauty, so his followers should live simply in their God-given beauty. He remembers warning them that if they become too concerned about how much they possess or how they appear to others, they will lose their souls.

With these memories in mind, Jesus then gazes into the women's clothing section of a large department store. He sees row upon row of fashionable items: belts, blouses, bras, bust enhancers, girdles, jewelry, jumpers, leggings, lingerie, nightgowns, nightshirts, pajamas, panties, pants, pantyhose, robes, scarves, shirts, athletic shoes, casual shoes, dress shoes, evening shoes, sandals, shorts, skirts, socks, suits, sweaters, t-shirts, tank tops, tights, vests, waist shapers, wallets, watches, windsuits, and wraps. He watches as shoppers stroll through the aisles. He can't quite believe that people need, or rather want, so many different types of clothing. He wonders if women and men alike aren't being duped by advertisements into thinking that if they are to find lasting happiness in their lives, they must "dress well."

He then looks in the hallway of the mall and sees children hopping into the lap of Santa Claus. All are telling Santa what they want for Christmas. He realizes that these children have imbibed the attitudes of their parents. The children, too, think that "Christmas" is about "getting stuff."

His heart is not judgmental. Indeed, he is touched by the children. He knows that there is a place in life for having fun and playing with toys. He dimly remembers a toy his mother and father gave him. His heart is also touched by the parents. He knows that many of them mean well in wanting to buy things for their children. They want their children to be happy, and they think that if their children "get stuff," they will be happy. He knows that their intentions are good, even though they are confused about how to be good parents. *Forgive them,* he says to himself. *They know not what they do.*

Still, his heart is broken. He had truly hoped for a different kind of world. He had hoped that children might learn to enjoy the simple material things in life, but also to realize that the most important things in life are things like friendships and shared meals and the spontaneous self-growing of lilies. He had hoped that the adults might realize that their true worth does not lie in being well-dressed and attractive, rich and famous, but rather in being wise, compassionate, and inwardly free. *Something has gone wrong,* he says to himself. *What shall I do?*

Lawrence Ferlinghetti tells us. In a poem called "Christ Climbed Down," he says that Christ descended from his cross and ran to "where there are no rootless Christmas trees hung with candycanes and breakable stars," to where "no Sears Roebuck creches complete with plastic babe in a manger" arrived by parcel post, to where "no televised Wise Men" sang the praises of brand-name whiskey, to where "no fat handshaking stranger in a red flannel suit" bore sacks of gifts from Saks Fifth Avenue.

Christ did not run away to a distant location. Rather, he softly stole away into the very hearts of the people, where he could continue to whisper the possibility of a simpler and more loving way of living. Ferlinghetti puts it this way:

> Christ climbed down
> From His bare tree
> this year
> and softly stole away into
> some anonymous Mary's womb again
> where in the darkest night
> of everybody's anonymous soul
> He awaits again
> an unimaginable
> and impossibly
> Immaculous Reconception
> the very craziest
> of Second Comings[9]

From the vantage point of this book, Ferlinghetti is right. And this in two ways.

A Crazy Second Coming

First, he is right to say that Christ is within each of us, Christian and non-Christian alike, awaiting birth in our lives. By "Christ" I do not mean the historical Jesus. Rather I mean what the New Testament calls the "the Spirit of God" or, alternatively, "the Spirit of Christ." I mean God's prayer within us, God's sighing within us, God's Breathing. This Breathing is not satisfied with just being present in our hearts. It wants to be enfleshed in our lives and in the world.

Given this meaning of Christ, each of us is Mary, quite apart from whether we are Christian. If God was free to work in the heart of a young Jewish woman, God is also free to work in the heart of a Buddhist, Hindu, Muslim, or agnostic. What is most important, even for the Christian, is not that people become attached to their religious self-identities. It is not that they become attached to the saying "I am a Christian" or "I am a Jew" or "I am a Buddhist" or "I am a Muslim." It is that they—we—become Marys to the world, whether we are female or male. To "become Mary" is to listen to God's Breathing within us, respond to it, and help the Spirit of Christ become enfleshed in the world.

People can "become Mary" in different ways. In the first two chapters I offered two examples. In the first chapter I told the story of a young woman suffering from anorexia who experienced the indwelling Christ as a call to break free from compulsive thinness. As she took the first painful bite of food and accepted the love of others, she became Mary. The Spirit of Christ shone through her life. And in this chapter I have told the story of an older woman, needful of rest, who experienced the indwelling Christ as a call to take a walk in the woods, gaze into the eyes of a grasshopper, and discover her own "wild and precious life." As she gazed into the enormous and complicated eyes of the grasshopper and realized her kinship with all creatures, she too became Mary.

My point is that, at every moment of our lives, God's Breathing is within us as a fresh possibility for wisdom, compassion, and inner freedom, relative to the immediate circumstances at hand. I cannot know what God's call is for you, because I am not in your shoes. You cannot know what God's call is for me, because you are not in mine. Each of us will be called by God's Breathing, by the indwelling Spirit of Christ, in a different way.

Still, I imagine that you and I alike jointly experience the Spirit of Christ in at least one common way. Inwardly, we experience this Spirit as a call to say yes to what truly matters in life and no to the more questionable dimensions of consumer culture. This is God's prayer within each of us: that we be authentic and therefore true to our deepest potential as human beings.

And here, it seems to me, Ferlinghetti is right on a second matter. Every time we respond to God's prayer within us, a Second Coming does indeed occur. This Second Coming is not a cosmic event in which Jesus descends from the heavens, although, in some mysterious way, that event may occur. It is a momentary event in which the Spirit of Christ is enfleshed in our daily lives. Such Second Comings are indeed "crazy" from the vantage point of consumer culture. Consumerism tells us that the real world is dependent on greed, envy, and acquisitiveness, and that we are being foolish if we live otherwise. Christ tells us that the real world is rooted in God's love. In order to truly respond to God's prayer, then, within us, we must become a little "crazy" ourselves. We must be in the world but not of it. We must discover an inner freedom—a wildness and preciousness—that is counter-cultural and hence counter-consumerist. We must become, as Paul put it, "fools for Christ."

Hidden in Christ

Part of being a fool for Christ involves rediscovering the image of God within ourselves. The fool for Christ has the inner freedom to be unnoticed, to be "hidden with Christ in God," as Paul puts it in Colossians (3:3). This capacity to be hidden—to be quietly obedient to the call of each moment without needing to be noticed in that obedience—is nourished by the fact that the fool for Christ is in touch with a deeper and divine image, with what we might call a second and hidden face. Here an explanation is in order.

It seems to me that each of us is born with two faces. One is the face we see in the mirror, which grows and changes over time. I have watched my own visible face change over the years, and I am sure that you have as well. The other is the face of God within our hearts. Sometimes the first face—the one we see in the mirror—gets the best of us. When we get up in the morning and look in the mirror, it is sometimes tempting to ask: Do I measure up? Am I attractive enough? Am I successful enough? Am I famous yet? This is the nature of consumer culture. It encourages us to identify with the face we see in the mirror and to measure our lives by appearance, affluence, and marketable achievement.

Nevertheless, we sometimes awaken to the second face: the image of God within our hearts. A baby is born, a loved one dies, a marriage occurs, a friend needs help, and something goes wide in our hearts. This widening of our hearts is an activity of the second face. Indeed, it is God within us. For God is a Wideness within which the universe unfolds, and we are made in the image of this wideness. As a popular hymn puts it, there is a wideness in God's mercy, as wide as the sea. Within each of us, there is a drop of this oceanic mind.

Of course, this drop of divinity—this sky-like mind within each of us—is not a face in any usual sense. We cannot see it in the mirror. Its hair cannot be out of place. Its clothes cannot be out of fashion. It does not require cosmetic surgery. It does not really grow old.

Nevertheless, it is filled with new life, with what one one poet, Gerard Manley Hopkins, calls the "freshness deep down."[10] Other people can feel the presence of our true face—of our freshness deep down—when we love them, care for them, listen to them, laugh with them, and cry with them. They likewise sense its energies when we face suffering with courage, delight in beauty, seek truth for its own sake, and surrender to life's mystery. They say that in these moments we are living with integrity: with wisdom, compassion, and inner freedom. And they are right. In these moments we are indeed living in a deeper way. We are living from the center of our existence and the Center of the universe. We are living from God's Breathing. We are participating in the craziest of Second Comings.

Strangely, one of the blessings of this craziness—this holy foolishness—is that it frees us from being so concerned about what others think of us, and thus we enter into a deeper happiness than consumerism usually recognizes. We do not have to be famous. We have a deeper sense of security. Even if we are not Christian—even if we are just taking a walk in the woods and saying no to the prospect of feeling guilty about it—we are hidden in Christ. This capacity to be hidden, to be unknown and not worry about it, is a counter-consumer option. It means it's all right not to be famous.

A first step in realizing this all-rightness—this deeper happiness that comes in not being famous—is simply to recognize that we are lucky to be alive and to live from this luckiness. It is to this sense of luckiness, which Christians call grace, that I turn in the next chapter.

Chapter Three

Lucky, Lucky Life
Spirituality as Openness to Grace

Lucky life is like this. Lucky there is an ocean to come to.
Lucky you can judge yourself in this water.
Lucky the waves are cold enough to wash out the
meanness.
Lucky you can be purified over and over again.
Lucky there is the same cleanliness for everyone.
Lucky life is like that. Lucky life. Oh lucky life.
Oh lucky lucky life. Lucky life.

Gerald Stern[1]

And for all this, nature is never spent;
There lives the dearest freshness deep down things.
Gerard Manley Hopkins[2]

The general thesis of this book is that if we are to make the best of our wild and precious lives, we will need to say yes to the mystery of life and no to the various temptations of consumerism. One of these temptations is to believe that we are all on our own, that everything depends on whether we are a "success" or "failure" in life, and that being successful means "being attractive" and "making money" and "being accomplished in the marketplace."

I recommend instead that we recognize that there is an ultimate mercy in life—a deeper grace—in terms of which "success" and "failure" as defined by consumer culture are quite irrelevant. I want to call this deeper grace the luckiness of being alive.

Lucky, Lucky Life (Even When Things Are Horrible)

Not surprisingly, a recognition of this luckiness does not come easily in our age of consumerism. To be sure, consumerism does speak of a luck we can enjoy if we win the lottery. But it always encourages us to compare ourselves with others who seem luckier because they have more consumer goods or better figures, because they have bigger houses or higher salaries. In so doing, it creates a culture of envy, not gratitude. It neglects the deeper luckiness—a pure grace—that lies at the heart of reality.

This grace is not an idea we entertain in our heads or a condition that is imposed on us from the outside. Rather, it is a living gift—like fresh bread, or fresh air, or fresh water—that lies within us yet deeper. It is to this luckiness that the poet Gerald Stern points in the passage above when he says, "Lucky life. Oh lucky life. Oh lucky lucky life."

Stern's words are playful, childlike, and extravagant. It is fun to say them aloud, like a mantra or chant. A grace chant. But perhaps they are also a little embarrassing to adults, who are all too aware of the darker sides of life. And such extravagant language does not come easily to us, because we too often feel inhibited by the armor of envy. Still, the words are psalmlike and true, worthy of being included in any sacred scripture. Let's try them out. Let's chant the grace mantra.

Let's say that we are indeed lucky to be alive, not only when things are going well for us and for those we love, but also when we are sad and lonely, or mean and bitter.

Let's assume further that our luckiness does not lie in the circumstances we face, which can be fortunate or unfortunate, deserved or undeserved. Instead, let's recognize that bad things do happen that could and should have been otherwise. Earthquakes kill thousands; people are murdered; children are abused; good people are nailed to crosses. Sometimes we ourselves are the nailers.

Let's say instead that our luckiness lies in a capacity to respond creatively to these circumstances, day by day and moment by moment, in fresh and healing ways. If we are sad, for example, we can lie gently with our sadness and let time begin its healing. If we are mean, we can be honest about our meanness and let honesty wash our souls. If we have nailed someone to a cross, we can ask for forgiveness. If we have ourselves been nailed, we can choose to forgive.

Let's go further. Let's assume that in these creative responses we are inwardly animated by a source of wisdom and compassion deep within nature that is forever fresh and new, however stale we might feel. Let's say that there is a Freshness Deep Down. Let's call it God.

Perhaps better, let's call it God's *Breathing,* since the Freshness is dynamic and nourishing, like breathing itself. Let's say that this divine Breathing is everywhere in the universe such that there is nowhere we can go, not even to hell, where it is not already present, awaiting our openness to its healing power.

Let's say that this, then, is why we are so lucky to be alive. It is not that everything happens as it should or that we always do the right thing. It is that, whatever happens and whatever we do, there is always hope for us and for all living beings. We can be animated by the Freshness. We can be breathed by the Breathing. We can be washed by the Ocean. We can live from the Center.

Here the Center is not the private ego with its encrusted self-images, but rather the Freshness Deep Down. It is the Luckiness within life. It is God's Breathing. By God I mean a spacious receptacle—an Open Space—within which the entire universe unfolds, moment by moment. Always we are within the deeper Mystery—the Open Space—that embraces us with a tender care that nothing be lost.

For good or ill, we can never draw a circle around this Embrace or place it within a frame. Often we try. We create theologies and philosophies that try to box in the Mystery as if it were a puzzle to be solved. In truth it is quite different. It is a Mystery to be felt, not a puzzle to be solved. This Mystery is immanent on our small planet as our own inner wisdom and as a healing energy that shines through plants and animals, hills and rivers, trees and stars, spirits and ancestors. Yet it is also transcendent as a wider context—an ultimate mercy—within which all things unfold. It is a circle whose center is everywhere and circumference nowhere.

We live from the Center when we are open to the breathings and washings of this Mystery—this Open Space—and when we are trustful that, no matter what happens, we are welcomed into its ultimate mercy. This trust is what many Christians mean by "faith in God." And the openness is what Christians call "being open to the Holy Spirit." But the phrases are not really important. What is most important is that people live from the Center, each in his or her own way and each in his or her own tradition.

The question is, Where do we begin? I think that one place we begin is simply to recognize a desire for happiness that lies within each human being: a desire that all beings be happy, each in her or his own way. It is to this subject—that of happiness—that I now turn.

May All Beings Be Happy: A Buddhist Prayer

"What is happiness?" I was slightly surprised by the question. It came from an exchange student from Africa who was taking a course under me. We were talking in the hallway after a class one day, during which she had learned that Americans speak of the pursuit of happiness as a God-given right.

She had two questions. She wondered whether "happiness" meant "pleasure" or "contentment" or "joy" or "peace of mind." And she wondered if we Americans didn't work a bit too hard pursuing these states of mind.

Of course, I use the word *happiness* often, and sometimes prayerfully. One of the most meaningful prayers I know comes from a Buddhist scripture called the Metta Sutra. It reads,

> May all beings be happy.
> May they live in safety and joy.
> All living beings, whether weak or strong,
> tall or stout, medium or short,
> seen or unseen, near or distant,
> born or not to be born,
> may they all be happy.[3]

I like this prayer. I myself am one of the medium-height beings for whom Buddhists are praying.

To be sure, in a Buddhist context, this prayer is not addressed to God but rather to the universe or to the open future. Still, as a Christian, I think it is one of the deepest prayers we can offer to God, who is indeed that Open Space that contains the universe and the open future. In any case, I trust that the prayer for happiness is one of God's deepest prayers for us. In the Bible we find this prayer in the image of a messianic age, desired by God as well as by humans, in which all beings—even the lion and the lamb—will lie down together in peace and joy. I suspect that deep within each human heart there is this messianic hope that all beings will be happy. In this sense we are all Jews, even if we happen also to be Christians or Buddhists.

When we awaken to this hope for a messianic age—when *all* beings will be happy—we are awakening to God within us: that is, God's lure toward healing and wholeness, not just for ourselves, but for all creatures. Thus, God is praying within us all the time, and

God's prayer is that we all be happy. Even God is praying for the messianic age, and it is up to us to help bring it into reality.

Still, when asked by my student about the meaning of happiness, I wasn't quite sure how to answer. So I looked it up in an *Oxford English Dictionary* that I keep in my office and discovered that "happiness" has several meanings, none of which are normative. Alexander Pope puts it well: "Oh Happiness! Our being's end and aim. Good, pleasure, ease, content! Whatever thy name."[4]

I shared Pope's saying with my student, thinking the matter was over, when, with a wide and engaging smile, she asked a follow-up question: "If Americans are always pursuing happiness, why aren't you Americans always happy?"

I knew that she was teasing me. We talked often about life in America and life in Africa, comparing and contrasting our two cultures. I knew that she really liked America and Americans. She was glad to be an exchange student. But I also knew that she had criticisms of America. One thing she liked about villages in Africa was that people enjoy a slower and more natural rhythm in life; they are not so enslaved to getting things done. So I said to her, "Why do you think we Americans are not always happy?"

She said in response, "Sometimes I think you Americans are not so happy because you are so busy trying to be happy. You go here and there, doing this and that, always looking for happiness. Maybe you ought to stop pursuing happiness and just let it come."

Her remark struck me as exceedingly wise. As a Christian, I believe in divine grace. I have the suspicion that true happiness is not something we acquire by pursuing, but rather something that comes to us, like truly good luck, when we let go of our obsessions with pursuit. So I began to think about the pursuit of happiness in America. Why had this student decided that, all things considered, we Americans were not so happy? Was she right? Should we stop pursuing happiness and just let it come?

With these questions in mind, I offer five observations concerning happiness, which you might reflect on in your own way, testing them against your own observations concerning happiness in America. They are:

- Happiness has three sources: meaningful work, healthy social relations, and leisure.
- Happiness is usually a byproduct of pursuing other ends, especially meaningful work and community with others, rather than an end in itself.

- Happiness is often inhibited by comparisons we make with others and by asking the question, Am I happy?
- Happiness, along with other emotions, can be contagious, because we "feel the feelings" of others, even when we are not aware of it.
- The deepest happiness is to live in the presence of God, which is itself the joy that Jesus shared with his disciples.

In terms of this book, the final observation is the most important. To live in the presence of God is to practice the presence of God and thus live from the Center, day by day and moment by moment. It is this kind of living that I see in Jesus and in others, including non-Christians, who participate in his Way. I think Jesus is right. I think it is the Way, the Truth, and the Life through which we come to God.

I think Buddhists are right too. Living from the Center does seem to be filled with the two qualities of happiness named in the Metta Sutra: safety and joy. It is safe in the sense that it provides inner peace, enabling us to respond to life's more difficult and dangerous circumstances with equanimity and strength. And it is joyful in that it includes a deep sense of creativity and wellness.

For now, however, I want to comment further on the first four observations, explaining how they are related to some problems we face in consumer culture. I think that consumerism may be one of the reasons Americans pursue happiness too much and, in the process, are not always very happy.

Three Contexts for Happiness: Work, Relationships, and Leisure

I borrow the first observation from Oxford University psychologist Michael Argyle, in his book *The Psychology of Happiness*. It is that three things make people happy in America or anywhere else in the world: (1) meaningful work, (2) healthy relations with family and members of one's community, and (3) opportunities for leisure, rest, and relaxation.[5]

The general idea is that if one or several of these are in place, people will report that they are happy, even if they do not have very much money or own very many possessions. If one or several are not in place, people will say that they are unhappy, even if they have a lot of money and own more than they need. Let us consider these three a little more carefully.

The question emerges, What is meaningful work? In America and in other parts of the world, it seems to me that meaningful work tends to be work (1) that gives one a sense of making a contribution to other people or to a larger whole or (2) that is interesting and exciting. If people are happy in their work, it is because one or both of these criteria are satisfied.

Of course, there are many people who are unhappy in their work by both these criteria. Consider a woman who works in an assembly line manufacturing a product—weapons or cigarettes, for example—of questionable service to society. Her work is not especially interesting to her, and it does not give her a sense of helping others. Nevertheless, she works for the wages she receives, hopeful that these wages will help her pay the bills and perhaps have some disposable income for leisure. In America, it seems to me, many people are in this situation. If they find happiness, it occurs at home and on weekends.

It is also worth noting that some people are happy in their work, primarily because it satisfies the second criterion noted above, not the first. They find happiness in their work because it is interesting and challenging, not because it gives them a sense that they are helping make the world a better place.

Consider a man who works for an advertising agency helping to produce advertisements that sell the products—weapons or cigarettes—being produced by the people named above. He often finds himself exhilarated by the creative energy involved in producing the ads, but he does not (and perhaps cannot) pause and ask, "Are these ads worth producing in the first place? Are they really good for people?" The very question would threaten his own sense of self-worth and threaten his position in the workplace.

What, then, is authentically meaningful work? I believe that it is work that satisfies the first criterion named above: It helps people, other living beings, and the Earth by promoting joy, reducing suffering, or creating beauty. The second criterion is then secondary rather than primary, like icing on a cake. On this measure, there is more good work in being a homemaker helping care for children than in the creativity of producing an ad for cigarettes.

The problem, of course, is that in a consumer society, good work is too often identified with having a job or being gainfully employed. When people ask others, "What do you do?" they usually mean, "What do you do outside the home for which you receive money?" If you answer, "I enjoy playing with my children, working in my garden, and watching birds," they respond, "Yes, but what do you do?" The solution to this problem is for attitudes to change—individual by individual, household by household, community by community, nation by nation— so that truly good work can be recognized for what it is: a source of deep delight in which our gladness meets the world's hungers, quite independently of financial reward. Toward this end, the media and the arts have an important role to play in offering nonconsumerist role models.

A word is also in order about the second source of happiness: healthy social relations. By healthy social relations I mean relations among friends, family members, neighbors, and co-workers in which there is intimacy, honesty, and mutual sharing, but also relations with other living beings and the Earth. Let "society" mean the Earth community, of which humans are a part, rather than the human community, for which the Earth is mere backdrop.

Of course, in America and in many parts of the world, many people are happy by virtue of their friendships and personal relationships. We need not exaggerate the degree of unhappiness in our world. Nevertheless, it is worth noting that in consumer society, with its emphasis on "having a successful career" and "paid work," people are often too busy and harried to have optimum relations with spouses and children. This is especially true for those who work outside the home eight to ten hours a day and who also find themselves responsible for domestic work. Often, by virtue of patriarchal social relationships, they end up carrying the lion's share of two jobs, one outside the home and one inside the home, and are then too tired or stressed to enjoy family relations. Put simply, consumerism is tough on children and marriages. It would be much better for families and children if society were organized around helping families rather than growing the economy.

Consider also the third source of happiness: leisure and relaxation. Here, too, let us not exaggerate. Many people find it easy to relax and enjoy. But it is worth noting that the atmosphere of busyness and speed, characteristic of consumer society in an information age, often makes it difficult for some people to slow down and relax, even when they are supposed to be relaxing. They—we—go on vacation, but we are then too busy trying to have fun to have fun. Or we wait for a weekend to relax, only to discover that, once the weekend arrives, we are still in a hurry.

This problem of being hurried is intensified by the rise of information technologies and mass communications, which lead us to be impatient with slowness and fearful of boredom. We must always be entertained by something new or else we are not having fun. And if our computer is too slow, we must get a faster one. As a result of these influences, many of us are not very good relaxers. We are habituated to being busy all the time in our lives, both by the culture of the workplace and the atmosphere of an information age, and it is not easy for some of us to recover the arts of "sitting still" and "simply enjoying."

The point can be put biblically. We recall that on the seventh day of creation, God did not do anything, but rather relaxed in the simple enjoyment of a creation that was very good. With its emphasis on activity, consumer society is hostile to sabbath consciousness, even as it is hostile to family life. God may have relaxed on the seventh day, but we still need to go shopping and get things done.

Happiness as Byproduct, Not Goal

The second general proposal concerning happiness derives from Holocaust survivor Victor Frankl in *Man's Search for Meaning*. His book draws from the experiences of prisoners in concentration camps and shows how, in the extremities of their situation, those who survived were the ones who had a goal in life rather than the ones who pursued happiness as an end in itself.[6] This proposal is that, while happiness may be part of what makes a life worth living, it is not really an end in itself, but rather a byproduct of other aims. In the words of my African student, happiness happens to us when we are not necessarily looking for happiness.

Three insights follow from Frankl's point. The first is that we ought not spend too much time pursuing happiness. It is much better to give ourselves to praiseworthy ends, such as service to others or the creation of beauty in the world, and then let happiness come, if it does.

The second insight is that many people can live very meaningful lives, pursuing quite worthy goals, without being particularly happy, if "happiness" means pleasant states of consciousness. Consider the person who is deeply compassionate, sharing in the sorrows of others, and who, precisely through her sharing, cannot sleep well at night. In her empathy for others, she knows the happiness of communion with others, but not the happiness of pleasure. In this communion there is deep meaning and perhaps even joy. But the joy at issue is not reducible to pleasure and can itself coincide with deep pain. It is a deeper form of happiness.

The third insight we gain from Frankl is that some of the unhappiest people in the world may be those who seek happiness as an end in itself, rather than allowing it to be a byproduct of nobler ends. In their pursuit of happiness they fall into the unhappiest of situations. They are living only for themselves.

Of course, Frankl's point can be overstated. It seems to me that for many if not all people, it is indeed appropriate in some contexts to pursue happiness, including pleasant states of consciousness. Consider people who are depressed and who want to be happy. Surely there is a place in life for their desire. Surely it is to happiness, forthrightly pursued, that God calls them.

Consider also people in lesser straits, who sometimes simply want to have fun. For my part, I believe that some of God's aims for us, some of the time, are for fun, pure and simple. We go out to have a good time, and it is precisely that good time that God wants for us. Even Jesus enjoyed a good party.

Still, there is truth in Frankl's point. If God wants each and every creature on the planet to be happy, it does not necessarily follow that God calls each creature to pursue happiness as an end in itself. Rather, God calls each creature to pursue worthy goals relative to each situation, some of which are for work and some for play, some for communion and some for solitude, some for love and some for beauty. The moment-by-moment calls from God—the fresh possibilities for healing and wholeness that we discover in discernment—are the goals worth pursuing. This means that, in a general way, we best understand our task as "obedience to the divine call of the moment" rather than "the pursuit of happiness." In this obedience, happiness will come as a byproduct.

Unfortunately, consumer society does not see things this way. Often we are told by the advertisements (1) that happiness is indeed an end in itself, rather than a byproduct of meaningful living, (2) that happiness is reducible to pleasant states of consciousness, and (3) that the sole aim worthy of our commitment is to enjoy consumer goods and services. Thus, we find ourselves seeking pleasant states of consciousness as ends in themselves, inspired by people who seem to enjoy more pleasure than the rest of us.

The mass media is particularly responsible for conveying this outlook on life. It presents images of celebrities with perfect smiles, indicative of perfect pleasure, to which we aspire. If we buy this beer or drive this car, we can then be completely happy like them. In the process of this insatiable drive toward self-validation, we end up dissatisfied with our own lesser smile, however finite but beautiful it might be.

Happiness as Relative, Not Absolute

The third observation is that, for many if not most people, happiness is relative. Or, to be more precise, happiness is partly the result of conscious and unconscious comparisons between "how we are doing" and "how others are doing." If other people seem "happier" than we are, we are then less happy and somewhat envious. If other people seem "unhappy," we are then happy that we are not as unhappy.

Here, too, consumer society often makes matters worse, because it constantly invites comparisons, not only with people we know but also with people we do not know. These include people modeled in advertisements on radio and television and displayed in the media. Thus, people compare themselves with celebrities, television personalities, and people who are inordinately rich, as well as to close friends and neighbors. Precisely because these others seem so happy in their glamour, the comparisons are often negative. They say to themselves, "I am not as happy as the man in the advertisement is, but if I buy this product, I might just become happier." The point is that, in the age of consumerism, advertisements and mass media play an unrestrained role in producing the standards by which happiness is assessed.

Happiness as Contagious

The next observation—that happiness can be contagious—is more positive. It derives not only from personal experience, which so often suggests that we are influenced for good and ill by the moods and emotions of those around us, but also from process theology, which proposes that the universe is an interconnected web of life and that all living beings "feel the feelings" of one another in varying ways and degrees.

Here I am reminded of the great work of the late Quaker writer Howard Thurman. Thurman was the grandson of slaves, and his grandmother, a former slave, reared him. In explaining how religious experience can be, in his words, "contagious," he recalls how, when he was a boy, his grandmother used to tell the story of hearing a Christian minister, himself a slave, inspire fellow slaves amid their fear of the slave owners. "How everything in me quivered with the pulsing tremor of raw energy when, in her recital, she would come to the triumphant climax of the minister: 'You—you are not niggers. You—you are not slaves. You are God's children.'"[7]

Thurman then explains how, when his grandmother said this, he himself felt the sense of dignity and joy that his grandmother felt. He felt her feelings, and he felt dignified himself. In this sense, so he explains, a religious experience—in this case a deep sense of self-worth—can be contagious. It can be transmitted from one person to another through shared feeling.

And so it is with many kinds of feelings, religious and otherwise. We humans are not skin-encapsulated egos, cut off from others by the boundaries of our skin. Rather, we are living cells with permeable membranes, continually receiving from others not only objective sensations of color and sound but also inner emotions that others are feeling. We are inwardly composed not only of our feelings but also, in varying degrees, of the feelings of others: humans, to be sure, but also other living beings.

From an inner perspective, this means that the deepest level of our own immediate experience—beneath words and concepts and beneath even sight and touch—is empathy: that is, a feeling of the feelings of others. We are open to the feelings of others at a subconscious level, even if we feel anaesthetized or cut off from their feelings at a more conscious level.

True, we can never feel the feelings of others as they themselves feel them. I cannot feel your suffering as you yourself feel it; nor can I feel your joy in this way. I always feel the feelings of others from my perspective: from the vantage point of where I am sitting or standing, in light of what I have experienced in my own past, as colored and shaped by my own moods and opinions, beliefs and preoccupations. From the perspective of process theology, the bottom line of human experience is empathy, but not necessarily perfect and un-perspectival empathy. In a sustained and ongoing way, such perfect empathy belongs only to God, who is that Deep Empathy within the heart of reality: equally present to all living beings. I myself am not equally present to all living beings. I know less of the amoeba than I know of a fellow human, and this will probably always be the case, perhaps until my own body drops away. This is what makes God "God." Devoid of a localized body, God is present to all things equally. The universe itself is God's body.

Envy as Contagious Too

Nevertheless, in this life we do indeed feel the feelings of others, and this is both bad news and good news. On the bad news side, it means that we share in the envy, hatred, and jealousies of others, such that their sins and our own cannot be sharply separated.

Consumer culture is itself a community of communal envy in which the envy of one person contributes to the envy of another, intensifying the envy of each. On the good news side, it means that we share in the sorrows and sadnesses of others, such that they need not be entirely alone in their pain. And it means also that we can share in their joys, such that our sadnesses can be partly alleviated by their joys if we are free from envy. And it means that they can share in our joys, too, such that, even if they are very sad, they can receive some of our joy. I suspect that this is the very way that Jesus transmitted joy to his disciples. It was not through his teachings; it was through his inner condition.

This experience of receiving joy from one another is fairly commonplace. All of us have people in our lives who, through their good spirit and happiness, just "make us happy" when they enter the room. It is not that they are perfect. Indeed, people who seem too perfect to us—who always do the right thing—do not usually make us happy. Envious or admiring, but not happy. Rather, it is that these joy-givers are human, just like us, with good features and bad features. Howard Thurman's grandmother was like this. In her inner peace, in her deep gladness, her joy was contagious to her grandson. As he puts it, he caught her joy, not unlike the way in which another person might catch the measles.

Such, then, is my fourth point. It is that happiness, including its deepest forms, can be contagious. This means that what the world sorely needs today, in our age of consumerism, are people who are deeply happy, not by virtue of appearance, affluence, and achievement, but by virtue of wisdom, compassion, and inner freedom. It needs people who live from the Center and whose joy in such living is contagious.

At a public level, we already have some icons of happiness. They are Mother Teresa[8] and the Dalai Lama. It is interesting to note that when people are in their presence, they often feel happy, even if prior to that they were quite sad. Mother Teresa and the Dalai Lama belong to the whole of the world, not just to Christianity and Tibetan Buddhism. They are vessels for God's Breathing in the world.

But the real need is not only for counter-consumer icons such as these two saints. It is for each of us, in small and humble ways, given all our finitude, to become vessels of happiness as well, through which other people, and other living beings, find safety and joy. As this happens, the world grows just a bit closer to that messianic state for which even God rightly prays. It grows just a little closer to that time when, as the Metta Sutra puts it, *all* beings will be happy: weak or strong, tall or stout, medium or short.[9]

As Frankl reminds us, the way to become a vessel for happiness is not necessarily to pursue happiness as an end in itself. Here Mother Teresa is a model. Her aim in life was not to become happy. It was to serve Jesus by serving the poorest of the poor. In this service, she became a person filled with joy. Here the Dalai Lama is also a model. His aim is not to arrive at or dwell in enlightenment, but rather to help make others happy, thus fulfilling his bodhisattva vow.

And so it is with us. If we seek to live from the Center, it is not for our sakes alone or for our sakes primarily. It is for the sake of the universe itself, that greater whole of which we are a part. For some of us, this can best be understood as service to a man whose face is seen in every person who is poor and powerless: namely, Jesus. Like Mother Teresa, we will serve Jesus by serving the world. This is the way of the Christian.

For others, it will be best understood as obedience to the creator and sustainer of the universe. This is the way of many Jews and Muslims. And for still others, it will best be understood as service to the universe itself. This is the way of many Buddhists.

When we enter into such service, we are no longer so dependent on comparing ourselves with others and asking, "How happy am I compared to them?" It is enough to do our best and then to share in the joys and sufferings of others. And we are also not so dependent on finding happiness in the three sources named earlier: meaningful work, healthy social relations, and opportunities for leisure. If we are fortunate enough to have meaningful work, it is a great joy in life. Our work then becomes a means through which our service might be expressed. And if we are blessed with friends and family, it is likewise a great joy. We meet God in the faces of our children and spouses and friends. Similarly, if we enjoy opportunities for leisure, they can be moments of sacramental awareness, of resting softly in the present moments of our lives.

But even if we are lacking these three conditions, we can nevertheless be happy in the deeper sense of contentment. Even if we are unemployed or unloved or busy. Our contentment comes from a deeper Center, which is itself more than a "good job" and a "happy family" and a "vacation." It comes from the Freshness Deep Down from which our lives emerge, moment by moment. It comes from God.

In order to live from God's Breathing, we begin by recognizing something that can sound provocative and even blasphemous, given the willful nature of consumer society. It is that we are lucky to be alive, quite apart from questions of failure or success, quite apart from how happy or unhappy other people seem to be, and quite apart from questions of appearance, affluence, and achievement. The question then becomes, How can we turn away from the shallower forms of happiness offered by consumerism and turn into the deeper form of happiness we see in Jesus and the Buddha, Mother Teresa and the Dalai Lama? How can we turn into, and return to, a deeper participation in pure grace?

Four Steps toward a Deeper Happiness

Earlier I suggested that an important step is simply to quiet down and listen to our own deepest hope, which is that all beings, ourselves included, be happy. Here let me recommend four correlative steps that can be taken simultaneously, the last of which is quite practical. They are, as it were, four steps toward deeper happiness. The first two are negative, and the second two are positive.

First, and perhaps obviously, we can accept our dissatisfaction with consumer culture and acknowledge our desire to live in a different way. We can reject the idea that appearance, affluence, and achievement are worthy values by which to live, and seek instead to live from wisdom, compassion, and inner freedom.

Second, we can try to be mindful of various ways in which consumerism influences our lives, unconsciously as well as consciously, guarding our hearts against further influence. We can speak back to those voices within us that say, *You are what you wear* and *You are what you earn* and *Your worth depends on your performance.* We can say no to these voices again and again, cognizant that they are the enemies of our better selves. Perhaps the ten temptations of consumerism, identified in chapter 1, can help toward this end.

Third, we can try to notice various ways in which God has already been breathing within us, despite the influences of consumerism. We can take take note of the many ways in which God is present in life, including the nine ways introduced in the first chapter: discernment, sacramental awareness (including holy communion and delight in beauty), openness to healing, living-by-dying, deep listening, trust in open space, courage in suffering, creativity, and loving-kindness.

Fourth and finally, we can willingly cooperate with God's Breathing in active and concrete ways. For the overconsumers among us, this will involve (1) lifestyle simplification, (2) obedience to a disciplined spiritual path of prayer and meditation, and (3) a regular offering of our time, energy, and action in service to others.

From the perspective of this book, the first step—a prioritization of values—is itself a response to divine Breathing in our lives. Our own desire to live more wisely and compassionately does not simply belong to us, but also to God. It is God's Prayer within us, God's hope that we make the best of our wild and precious lives. To accept this desire—to acknowledge that we want more than consumerism offers—is itself a way of responding to, and being animated by, the divine Breathing. It is saying yes to our own deepest hope for a whole and loving life. Even if we do not believe in God, our yes is God-breathed.

The second step—recognizing the negative influence of consumerism in our lives—is another way we can be open to divine Breathing. God's prayer within us is not only a desire for wholeness, it is also a call to honesty. When we are honest about our own compulsions and greeds, our own shortcomings and sins, our very honesty is the presence of divine Freshness. We gain distance from the compulsions and freedom to change.

For many of us the third step—noticing ways in which God has already been breathing in us, often without our knowing it—is the most important. We will begin to live from the Center by realizing that this living is not all up to us, because God has been breathing in us and around us, day by day and moment by moment, quite apart from our actions and intentions. God has been breathing in us in our moments of honesty and hope, courage and love, delight and discernment, creativity and letting go. We have likewise received the Breathing through the presence of friends and family, plants and animals, hills and rivers, planets and stars, and even those who frustrate us and harm us, whom we nevertheless manage to forgive. In relation to the Breathing, we have never been completely alone; we have always been supported.

This realization is radical and countercultural. To the extent that we truly notice God's Breathing within us and around us, we live in the world of consumerism, but we are not quite of it anymore. After all, consumerism says that we must struggle very hard all the time to "make things happen" and "acquire things," including something called "spirituality." It does not permit us to relax, to lie back and rest gently in God's love, celebrating the sheer beauty of what already is. The very recognition that we do not have to struggle quite so hard—that some of the most important things in life are pure grace—is a tremendous step in living more spiritually. In noticing God's Breathing in our lives and in the world, we begin to create a consumer-free zone within the depths of our hearts. From this open space, we can begin to cooperate with God's Breathing.

This cooperation—which is the fourth step—can be difficult or easy, but in either instance it needs to be willing rather than willful. By "willingness" I mean an inner spirit of saying yes to the mystery of life, day by day and moment by moment. And by "willfulness" I mean an inner spirit of trying to control or master that mystery. Practical activity that is cooperative with divine Breathing is willing, not willful. It is activity that seeks to cooperate with God's Breathing, all the while knowing that there is more to the Breath of Life—more to God's Breathing—than our experience can ever comprehend.

As noted above, the fourth step—cooperation with the Breathing—can take three forms: (1) lifestyle simplification, (2) obedience to a disciplined spiritual path of prayer and meditation, and (3) service to others. By lifestyle simplification I mean giving things away, buying fewer goods, and learning to appreciate the simple things in life, such as friendships and sunsets and walks in the woods. I mean choosing to work for less money in order to spend time with family and have time for volunteer work, wearing clothes that are functional rather than fashionable, and learning to let go of the need always to have more and more.

By obedience to a disciplined spiritual path I mean (1) a daily practice of prayer or meditation of, say, twenty minutes to an hour each day, in which we take a sabbath from work and activity, simply to say yes to God's Breathing in our own intimate way. Such obedience can involve yoga, Bible study, Zen meditation, journaling, active prayer, or some combination of all these. Such obedience can also be complemented (2) by periodic times of silent retreat for a weekend or a week, alone or with others, and (3) by regular visits with a spiritual director or spiritual friend, who seeks to help us be accountable to the deepest yearnings of God within our lives. Without such obedience, we tend to wander about, lacking a spiritual anchor to our daily lives and lacking the inner resources to move past consumerism in the long haul.

By service to others I mean activities as diverse as playing with children, taking care of the elderly, working in soup kitchens, baking bread for the aggrieved, working on political campaigns, cleaning up litter, planting trees, caring for animals, and helping others, human and nonhuman, in practical and loving ways. I mean doing the Great Work.

Such service is critical to authentic spiritual living, without which it lapses into spiritual narcissism. Nevertheless, as we enter into service, it is quite important that it be humble rather than prideful. Service best begins not with a preconceived agenda concerning what is good for others but with a quiet and nonjudgmental listening to these others, on their own terms and for their own sakes. This listening itself is one of the fundamental ways we can willingly cooperate with God's Breathing. It is one of the primary fruits of an attentive heart.

In our age of consumerism, this listening will not come easily. We are so easily distracted, not only by things happening outside us but also by chattering voices within us. In order to find our listening hearts, we will need obedience to a disciplined spiritual path; we will need spiritual disciplines that help us find a quieter side to our lives. One of the most important of these disciplines may well be fasting, not necessarily from food and drink, but from telephones, televisions, computers, and the Internet: fasting from electricity. This fasting is particularly important because so much of our activity in consumer culture is driven by a need for more and more sensory stimulation, at ever-increasing rates. One of the most important ways we can actively cooperate with God's Breathing is to slow down. It is to discover that one of God's deepest languages is silence.

Of course, the four steps are not magic. It is not that we will take them one night and then awaken the next morning to discover that we have totally transcended the values and lifestyle of consumerism. We will need to take them again and again; and often, after taking one step forward, we will then take two steps back. Still, they are practical and hopeful steps. They can help us recognize that the whole of life—the beauty and the horror, the failure and the success, the agony and the ecstasy—is embraced and engraced by a deep grace: the Luckiness of Being.

CHAPTER FOUR

Lying Gently in the Water
Spirituality as Living-by-Dying

I write this book as a recovering Christian fundamentalist. Webster defines *fundamentalism* as "a movement in twentieth century Protestantism emphasizing the literally interpreted Bible as fundamental to Christian life and teaching." This definition is helpful insofar as it points to a distinctive movement in American Protestantism, in which I have been a participant. Nevertheless, the definition is lacking in two ways.

In the first place, it ignores the fact that there are other kinds of fundamentalism: Christian and Buddhist, Republican and Democrat, scientific and romantic, atheistic and theistic, countercultural and consumerist. The dominant fundamentalism of our time is not Protestant or Christian; it is consumerist.

In the second place, the definition from Webster neglects mentioning the mindset or attitude that gives rise to these various fundamentalisms. Part of this mindset involves inordinate attachment to a set of beliefs, prompted by a desire to freeze reality, to foreclose novelty, to reduce life's unfolding mystery to a manageable, confinable commodity. But the mindset really goes deeper than this. It is also prompted by a desire to freeze the Mystery within and beyond life's mystery. Fundamentalism is not just a desire to freeze life. It is also a desire to freeze God.

In the Abrahamic religious traditions, freezing God is called "idolatry." It is to make a thing or a substance of something that is really a no-thing, or an Open Space. Most of us do not do this in straightforward fashion. We do not say to God, "I now wish to freeze

99

you, to make you a thing, like a piece of ice, that I can hold in my hand." Rather, we take something slightly more concrete—like the Bible, our family, our career, or our need for approval—and allow it to function as the ultimate center of our lives. We then have a center that is not the Center, a god that is not God. We freeze God by substituting finite things for Open Space.

Confessions of a Recovering Fundamentalist

For my part, I have been a fundamentalist since the day I was born. My mother was one of my first substitutes for divinity, along with my father, my sister, and a cocker spaniel named Patty. I had a divine quaternity: four spirits in one divinity. My guess is that God forgives me these idolatries and a host of others besides. After all, we need channels of grace in our lives. We need finite beings who are vessels of heavenly Wisdom. If sometimes we confuse the channels with the grace, or the vessels with the Wisdom, perhaps we are doing the best we can under the circumstances at hand. Surely God is patient with our confusions.

Still, some forms of idolatry are destructive, and we'd best recover from them, if not for God's sake, then for our own. I first became aware of my own capacities for more destructive fundamentalism at about age twenty, when I was a senior in college. My false god was called "Christianity." It might better be called "Christianism."

My Christianism began late one night when I was feeling a need to find direction in my life, to say yes to God. I realized that, for too many years, my own ego had been my "lord and savior," and it hadn't been doing a very good job. I was having trouble with friends and parents, with school and life. I wanted a new way of living: one that would help me become kind, and gentle, and free. And one that would give me permission to reject the materialism of American society and to live simply and frugally, in obedience to a path of compassion.

So late one night, in the quietness of my dormitory room, I sat down, pictured Jesus in my imagination, and asked him into my life forever. He was my way to Love.

I had friends who believed that this kind of action—a personal decision for Christ—was an example of idolatry. They saw Jesus as a crutch, not a savior. In retrospect, I think that they had a very good point. At least in some ways. These days, when I drive down the street and see Jesus advertised on billboards and license plates, I realize that he has become a fetish in many a Christian imagination. He has become a product—like aspirin—that is bought and sold in the marketplace, with Christians claiming ownership of the company that produces the product. Amid this, the real Jesus—the grace-filled Nazarene—has been lost. We Christians are pretty good at boxing in Jesus. We are pretty good at christolatry.

Still, when I was a senior in college, I'm not sure I lapsed into this form of idolatry. At least it didn't feel this way. The man to whom I entrusted my heart felt more like a window to the Divine than a box for the Divine. He was a departed Ancestor, a holy Icon, a living Master, but not a piece of ice.

Nevertheless, a false god entered my life at that time. It was a mental grid by which I tried to understand the commitment I had made to Christ and into which I attempted to fit even Jesus. It was my way of boxing him in, so that he became more manageable. I called my grid "Christianity."

I became aware of the grid late one night, about ten o'clock, when my next-door neighbor in the dorm, Lee, knocked on my door. Lee didn't know that I had become a Christian, because I hadn't told many people. Too many of the avowed Christians I knew in college were stuffy. I got to know them, but not publicly. They didn't drink beer or listen to the Rolling Stones. I was a little embarrassed to be associated with them.

Lee, on the other hand, was not a Christian. He was an ex–Southern Baptist. I liked him for this reason. It meant that he was open to fresh ideas and new possibilities. He thought of me as a soulmate, as someone with whom he could share. When he knocked on the door, I knew what he wanted. He wanted to talk, as always, about philosophy and religion.

"Jay," he said, "do you have a minute? Remember that course on Buddhism I told you I was taking? Well, it's great. Dr. King is teaching us about Zen, and it's really helping me. I think I'm rediscovering religion, or at least something spiritual. Can you listen?"

The problem was: I could *not* listen. Not that night. As Lee spoke, an almost bodily feeling came over me. It was one of disapproval, of nonacceptance, of judgment. From some conservative Christians, I had learned about the great commission in Matthew, where Christians are told to go unto all nations and make disciples. Influenced by them, the dormitory had become my nation, and Lee was among the disciples I was to make. Moreover, for me, at that time, a "disciple" was someone who believed as I believed, who recognized Jesus as God's only Son.

So instead of saying to Lee, "Tell me more. I'd love to listen," I said, "Lee, you need to know something about me. I've become a Christian. I think you're headed in the wrong direction. I think Zen is all wrong. I think Christianity is the only way. I think you ought to become a Christian too."

As I said this, it never occurred to me that the very God who had drawn me to Jesus might also have drawn Lee to Zen. It never dawned on me that my way to God was not the only way to God. Rather, I assumed, as do all fundamentalists, that my way was the only way, that my truth was the Final Truth.

It was with this episode, then, that my friendship with Lee began to end. He sensed, rightly, that I would no longer be able to listen to him and accept him on his own terms. From then on, I would have an agenda—called "Making Lee a Christian"—that would keep me from honoring his otherness, from sharing in his joy, from respecting his independence, from being his soul friend. The world had gained a Christian, but it had lost a listener.

As I ruminated on my encounter with Lee in the months thereafter, I was not really comfortable with who I had become. Influenced by the conservative Christians I'd been talking to, I thought that I was supposed to believe in the supremacy of Christianity and in the necessity of people's "becoming Christian" if they were to be acceptable to God. Intellectually, I assumed that if Christianity was right, other religions had to be wrong.

But inwardly, at a deeper level, I heard a different voice. Even as I was telling Lee to ignore Zen, I felt that I ought to be listening to him, hearing him on his own terms and for his own sake. Something in me was saying, *Listen to him, share in his journey, throw away your agenda, respect his otherness.* I felt that the real Jesus—the one to whom I had entrusted my own heart—wanted me to listen in this way. So I was presented with a dilemma. Which voice should I listen to, that of my head or that of my heart? I was faced with a need for what, I later learned, Christians call "discernment."

As most Christians know, discernment is an art, not a science. We have to listen to the voices within us and figure out which come from God, which come from our selves, and which come from the enemy of our better selves, otherwise called "the devil." In relation to Lee, I'm pretty sure I listened to the wrong voice. I don't know whether it was my ego or the devil, but I doubt that it was God's voice. But I didn't really have a theology that gave me permission to listen to such deeper feelings or to recognize God's truth in other religions. I had a theology of the head, not of the heart; of christology, but not Christ. And this theology had control of me. My attachment to it kept me from being the better self I wanted to be. It kept me from having an open heart, from being a pasture for gazelles.

Loving-kindness

I borrow the phrase "pasture for gazelles" from the thirteenth-century Islamic writer Ibn Al-Arabi. Describing what it is like to be open to God's love, Ibn Al-Arabi wrote,

> My heart is opened unto all forms. It is a pasture for gazelles, a cloister for Christian monks, a temple for idols, the Ka'ba of the pilgrim, the tablets of the Torah and the book of the Koran. I practice the religion of Love; in whatsoever directions its caravans advance, the religion of Love shall be my religion and my faith.[1]

His words capture something of that better self that I wanted to be many years ago and that I'd like to be still today. I would like to be a pasture for gazelles and a temple for idols.

By "gazelles" I mean the joyful and playful side of life, the side that elicits joy and gratitude. The "gazelles" of our lives include the spontaneous laughter of children, the gentleness of free-flowing streams, the companionship of good friends, and the beauty of animals at play. By "idols," on the other hand, I mean the violent and tragic side of life: the side that elicits our fear and trembling. Our "idols" include the terrible pain of children with cancer, the pollution of once-healthy rivers, the loss of love and loved ones, the pain of animals being slaughtered. The "idols" are those dimensions of creation that are unnecessarily painful, sometimes even horrible.

Ibn Al-Arabi's point is that, if we are to follow the religion of Love, our hearts must be wide enough to include both sides of life: the beauty and the horror. It is not that we desire the horror or that we pretend to ourselves that it was "meant to be." Even as we face the horror, we wish that it did not occur. Still, the horror is a part of our lives, just as the beauty is part of our lives. If we are to follow the religion of Love, our hearts must be wide enough to accept the joy and the suffering, the beauty and the horror, with wisdom, compassion, and freedom.

And this, I think, is what made Jesus "the Christ." It was not that he was biologically born of a virgin or that he performed amazing miracles. Rather, it was that his heart was so widened by God that he became a pasture for gazelles and a temple for idols. On the "gazelle" side of things, he exhibited great zest for life. He enjoyed eating and drinking with sinners; he took delight in the little children who came up to him, recognizing in them the very Reign of God. But he also knew the dark side of things. He wept in the garden of Gesthemane and then faced his own cross with terrified courage, forgiving even those who hammered the nails into his hands. He was "the Christ" because he absorbed the sins and sufferings, and also the joys, of those around him. In so doing he revealed, and became, God. He showed that even God is an Open Space: a pasture for gazelles and a temple for idols too.

For many of us, of course, the phrase "Open Space" can at first sound strange. Most of us are taught to think of God as a mind or an energy, as a person or a presence, but not as an Open Space. And certainly, when we address God in prayer, it feels as if God is a surrounding mind or presence who hears us as we pray and who responds in some way to what is heard. We do not often describe this surrounding presence as Open Space.

My suggestion, however, is that this personal presence, this living God, is indeed more like an Open Space than a deity among deities, even a supreme deity. This does not mean that it is impersonal. We can pray to the Open Space as Mother or Father, as Guide and Friend, and when we do so, Someone is listening. But this Someone is not a thing or a process we can grab onto with our hands or our minds. It is more like the sky we see above us, which is neither to the left or the right, but rather everywhere at once. God, I submit, is a sky-like Mind. Our need is to be available to God's Breathing.

Divine Congealings

In order to be available to this Breathing, many of us need congealings of the Open Space. My point is not that we need to grasp the Open Space as an object among objects, as we might grasp a pencil or a rock. Rather, it is that, at certain points in our lives, this Open Space can congeal into a more concrete form, all the while remaining spacious in its ultimate horizons. In these moments, living beings and other "objects" such as music or art can become vessels of the Breathing. They become "sacraments" or "holy icons."

In this book I have presented several examples of such congealing. In chapter 1, I told the story of the young student of mine who suffered from anorexia. As she sought help from other people who had suffered in a similar way, and as they listened to her story in nonjudgmental love, they, too, were holy icons for her. In their compassionate eyes, too, and also in their listening, there was holy light. Here there was a congealing of the Open Space.

In chapter 2, I offered the image of a woman who took a walk in the woods and discovered her wild and precious life by looking into the eyes of a grasshopper. In this moment the grasshopper was, for her, a holy icon. As she gazed into its enormous and complicated eyes, the woman was gazing into the eyes of what was, for her, a vessel of divine light.

Such examples can be multiplied a thousandfold. A small boy can be a congealing of the Open Space when we hear him laugh and enjoy his innocence. An old woman can be a congealing of the Open Space when we hear her stories and learn from her wisdom. A butterfly can be a congealing of the Open Space when we watch its wings flutter in the wind and are amazed by its fragile beauty. And a carpenter from Nazareth can be a congealing of the Open Space when he enters into a healing ministry, loving and forgiving others for even their most heinous sins.

I believe that the latter is what we Christians mean when we say "God became incarnate in Jesus." We mean that, in the healing ministry of Jesus, we see a deep manifestation—a congealing—of the Open Space. Historically, we Christians have been tempted to emphasize the outward appearance of this congealing and perhaps even the color of his blood on the cross. But in truth it is not his body or the color of his blood that inspires our devotion. It is the openness of his own heart. What makes Jesus "the Christ" for most of us is that he was— and still is—an open space for the world. In his openness, we see the openness of the Open Space; in his capacity to absorb the sins and sufferings of the world, we see the absorptive capacity of the sky-like Mind. Grateful for his compassion, we want to be open spaces ourselves. We want to follow Christ by sharing in his healing ministry.

Part of this healing ministry involved what Jesus did in his own life: his eating and drinking with sinners, his enjoyment of parties, his forgiveness. But part of this ministry involved his death on the cross and his resurrection on the third day. We follow Jesus by joining him in this death and resurrection, by learning to live-by-dying or live-by-letting-go, not just when we face physical death, but in each moment of our lives. Perhaps an illustration is in order. I borrow it from a poem called "First Lesson," written by Philip Booth.

Living-by-Dying

Imagine that you are a young girl learning to float. You live close to the ocean, and your father is taking you to the beach for your first lesson. He finds a shallow place in the water where the current is not very strong, and he walks you to where the water is just above your waist. Then he cups his hands underneath your head and tells you to lie back into the water.

"Soon," he says, "I'm going to let go of your head. Don't turn over; that's the way dead people float. Just relax and look up at the sky. Someday you will be in much deeper water, and you can remember this lesson that I'm teaching you. Now lie back and lie gently. The sea will support you."

At first you are afraid. You really don't want him to release your head, and you really don't trust the water quite yet. But you do trust your father; and if he says you can float, then you will give it a try. So you give him permission to let go, and, as he does so, you also let go of your fears. This letting go is like a dying; you feel almost as if you are falling into an abyss. But as you look up at the sky and relax your grip, a strange feeling of trust wells up in your heart. To your surprise, a miracle occurs. You float.[2]

Christianity teaches that most of us are in the situation of this girl at almost every moment of our lives. We live and move and have our being in the supportive Water of a mystery deeper than words, of God. And yet we are deeply tempted to hold on to our fears at the expense of trusting the Water. The purpose of life is to trust the Water.

If we are lucky, we have good teachers—like the girl's father—who gently teach us the art of trust. A friend can be such a teacher, but so can an experience of deep suffering, an occasion of profound joy, a beloved animal, a beautiful forest, or a dying savior. No matter how gracious our teachers, however, there is one thing they cannot do for us. They cannot take our place in the letting go, in the lying back and gently floating in the Water. This is something the girl understands. She knows that she has to let go of her fears, and only she can do the letting go. The same applies to most of us throughout our lives. At any given moment there is something within us—an inner compulsion, an inordinate attachment—that must drop away if we are to let the Sea support us. Like the girl in the water, we must undergo a process of living-by-dying.

At one level, living-by-dying is simply one among the several ways we can be breathed by God in our daily lives. There is much in the spiritual life that is neglected if we focus only on it, at the expense of attending to other spiritual dynamics. At another level, however, living-by-dying is foundational. We cannot really listen to others and share in their suffering, or delight in beauty and trust fresh possibilities, unless we are also able to take up our cross and follow Christ. This is one of the deepest wisdoms of Christianity. It is called "death and resurrection."

By death, then, I do not mean something that happens to us at the end of our lives, but rather something that happens throughout our lives, again and again. It is an interior movement of the soul: a "letting go" or a "falling away" of inner desires that have become compulsions in our lives and that therefore block our capacities for freedom, wisdom, and love. The Christian tradition calls these desires "inordinate attachments." Resurrection is, then, the welling up within us of wisdom, compassion, and interior freedom as these attachments fall away.

What, then, are these "inordinate attachments" that must drop away if we are to lie back and gently float in the waters of Spirit? According to John of the Cross, they are inner desires that are habitual and voluntary and involve approaching finite goods as if they were Infinite.[3] As a simple example, consider an inordinate attachment to food.

It is one thing to be healthily attached to food and another to be inordinately attached to it. We are healthily attached to food if, when we are hungry, we want to eat. By contrast, we are inordinately attached to food if, even as we regularly have plenty to eat, we nevertheless want more and more, almost all the time, in order to fill an empty place in our souls. Here, food takes the place of the Infinite in our lives. We cling to it, not in a natural way, but rather in hopes that it will satisfy a deeper yearning. For those among us in this situation, the problem is not the need to eat, which is natural, but rather the compulsion to eat, which is unnatural. Food has become our god and eating our form of worship. We are inordinately attached.

Food is a good example because it is so tangible. Other candidates for idolatry are equally telling. We can and do make idols of our families, our careers, our personal appearances, our political philosophies, and even our religions. In the house of idolatry, there are many mansions. We can speak of family-olatry, appearance-olatry, politics-olatry, and certainly religion-olatry.

In my view, however, the most fundamental idols in our lives are within us rather than outside us. They are not food, clothing, and shelter, or even families, jobs, and religions. Rather, they are legitimate psychological needs around which our lives are centered, and which have therefore become compulsions for us. Our more public idolatries to family and job are thus rooted in these deeper idolatries, over which, it can sometimes seem, we have little if any control. In what follows I name nine psychological needs that, for many of us, can easily become false gods. I borrow this ninefold scheme from a personality profile called the Enneagram, which literally means "nine points."[4] For me, the Enneagram, with its proposal that there are nine personality types, has functioned as a helpful tool for understanding inner compulsions.

Nine False Gods

One psychological need that can become a compulsion is the need to be perfect. This is a desire for orderliness and tidiness in life, for everything to be "right" and "proper" and "as it should be." This need has become a false god in our lives if, in bondage to it, we are unable to accept imperfections in others or, as is so often the case, in ourselves. Enslaved to our perfectionist ideals, we then walk through life with an inner resentment that the things of this world—our families, our careers, our lives—are "not right" and "ought to be different." We cannot laugh or forgive or accept life's delightful imperfections. "Perfection" has become our god.

A second is the need to be needed. This is the desire to serve others, to help them, to make them happy. It has become a false god in our lives if, in bondage to it, we are unable to recognize that we ourselves also have personal needs, and if we are unable to accept the fact that, sometimes, other people may actually need us to leave them alone. Enslaved to our need to be needed, we walk through life with the assumption that other people are always, and perhaps inevitably, in need of us. "Being needed" has become our god.

A third candidate for idolatry is the need to receive approval. This is a desire to be recognized for our achievements and to receive applause. It has become a false god in our lives if, in service to it, we are unable to risk the disapproval of others, to "do the right thing" even if it is unpopular, or to "do the right thing" without even being noticed. Enslaved to our need for recognition, we then walk through life unable to accept personal failures and in perpetual quest for applause. "Receiving approval" has become our false god.

A fourth is the need to be perceived as unique and special and sensitive. This is the desire to be recognized not so much for outer achievements as for inner sensibilities: for our intuitions, feelings, imagination, and sorrows. This need has become a false god in our lives if, in bondage to it, we find ourselves always controlled by our own feelings and unable to accept our ordinariness. We walk through life hoping that others will notice that our joys are just a little more joyful than those of others, our sufferings just a little more painful, and our intuitions just a little deeper. "Being sensitive" has become our false god.

A fifth possibility is the need to understand. This is the desire to have cognitive frameworks or mental grids by which we understand, and feel control over, the multiple data of the world. This need has become a false god in our lives if, in service to it, we find ourselves unable to accept the mysteries and ambiguities of life, the things that cannot easily be enframed within our conceptual boxes. We walk through life in a perpetual quest for new and better information and are perhaps unable to truly act in the world, because we never quite have enough information. "Being knowledgeable" has become our false god.

A sixth possible idol is the need to belong. This is the desire to be a member of a larger group, to enjoy the fruits of being a team player who works with others to contribute to the larger good. The group at issue may be people at work, people at church, or one's own family. Our need to belong to this group, to identify with it and give it our energy, has become a false god in our lives if we find ourselves expecting far too much of the group with which we identify and are therefore unable to stand back, criticize it, and recognize its inability to satisfy our deepest spiritual needs. "Belonging to the group" has become our false god.

A seventh possible idol is the need to avoid suffering. This is the desire to be happy, to enjoy pleasant experiences, to look on the bright side of things. Our need to avoid suffering has become a false god if, in service to it, we are unable to accept our own suffering or that of others and are unable to recognize genuine tragedy in life. We are always on our way toward new pleasures, never quite able to be honest to the sadder side of life. "Being happy" has become our false god.

An eighth possibility is the need to be in control. This is the desire to be "on top" of the circumstances of our lives and effective in shaping the lives of others. It is the need to be a powerful person who is efficient and effective, who can organize others toward good ends and "get things done." Our need to be in control has become a false god if, in service to it, we are unable to accept our own feelings of vulnerability and we find ourselves always needing to be "the leader" at home and in the workplace. "Being in control" has become our false god.

A ninth possibility is the need to be mellow and peaceful. This is the desire to be calm and unmoved by life's circumstances, to be inwardly centered. It has become a false god in our lives if, enslaved by it, we are unable to be engaged with others in free and passionate ways, if we are unable to accept their joys and sufferings, and perhaps even our own, with seriousness. We find ourselves always needing to "sit back" and take things in without ever really being engaged with life itself. When this happens, "being mellow" has become our false god.

Dark Nights

Throughout our lives, most of us are tempted by several of these idolatries. Perhaps one of them is our most persistent temptation: the one to which we gravitate most readily in times of stress and trial. Still, most of us fall into the other idolatries as well. Even as our most persistent compulsion may be a desire for approval, we may nevertheless be enslaved to a need for control. Our obsession with receiving approval is conjoined with a need to control those whose approval we seek. Psychologically, most of us are not monotheists but rather polytheists. We are typically enslaved to a cluster of false gods.

To make matters worse, our enslavements are as much unconscious as conscious. At a conscious level, we may believe that we are helping others in the interest of compassion, while at an unconscious level we are helping them in order to receive their approval. Often our deeper motivations are hidden from us.

Even as our motivations may be hidden, however, they can also be voluntary. This is because our freedom is not limited to conscious freedom. At an unconscious level, we are making decisions all the time. Consider dreams. As images appear to us, we are constantly deciding in unconscious ways how to respond to them: to laugh, to cry, to escape, to enjoy. In some dreams we can even influence the images to some degree, thus affecting the outcome of the dream. Or consider driving a car. As we drive to the store to get food, we stop at signs, cross intersections, put our foot on the brake, and accelerate in a habitual and unselfconscious way. In the act of driving, we are making decisions all the time—"Stop here" and "Go there"—but these decisions are not clear, distinct, or reflective. They are pre-conscious and instinctive.

My point, then, is that some of our own deeper motivations—to receive approval from others and to avoid suffering, for example—may be the result of habitual but voluntary decisions that we make at a pre-conscious level, again and again. The very fact that they are voluntary means that, in time and with the help of auspicious circumstances, they can be undone. But always, the undoing will involve a letting go, a dying.

The dying is never easy. When, for example, we are letting go of a person to whom we've been inordinately attached, or a job, or a religion, it can seem as if we ourselves are dying, almost physically. And sometimes, quite literally, physical displacement must occur. We must leave the person, or abandon the career, or let go of the religion. We undergo a period of darkness, of grief, of despair. We undergo a "dark night of the soul."[5]

But dark nights are not the whole story. There is also rebirth, new life. At least this is the teaching of Christianity. The Way of Christ does not bypass the cross, but it does not stop there either. On the other side of death, so we discover, is resurrection. Like death itself, resurrection is something that can occur in this very life, again and again, at ever deepening levels. It occurs every time we live from the Center rather than the periphery.

Letting Go into Love

Given its emphasis on freedom from inordinate attachments, Christianity is almost the exact opposite of consumerism. Consumerism tells us that the purpose of life is to be so deeply attached to material goods and services that we never have to say, "Enough." It is a religion, or excessive attachment, of deep clinging.

By contrast, Christianity teaches us that we become happy by sharing in the sufferings of others without hiding or running away and by delighting in the good things in life without clinging to them when they pass away. It is a religion of freedom from clinging and freedom for love. Sometimes it can seem as if these two are opposites, as if freedom from clinging and freedom for love are at odds with each other. But in truth they go together. The freer we are from holding on to things as if they were private possessions, the freer we are to love our neighbors on their own terms and for their own sakes and to love God in a similar way. The heart of Christianity is a letting-go-into-love.

Indeed, from a Christian perspective, the spiritual life is an ongoing process of death-and-resurrection—of letting-go-into-love—at ever deepening levels. There arc not necessarily stages to the spiritual journey; each person's is different. But there is spiritual growth, and this growth occurs in a lifelong process of letting go of false gods, dying ever more deeply each time, and thus being resurrected into deeper forms of wisdom, compassion, and freedom.

In the course of a lifetime, there are many false gods to which we must die, sometimes again and again. When I was a Christian fundamentalist, my false god was "the illusion of having the perfect set of beliefs" or "the illusion of thinking that I was right about everything." When this god reigns in our lives, we are inordinately attached to a worldview or ideology that makes sense to us and that may well contain great wisdom. We call it "the Gospel" or "the Dharma" or "the Truth" or "the Way Things Are." It is a discursive scheme, a verbal formula, in terms of which we try to ground our lives.

Of course, there is nothing wrong with discursive schemes. They are necessary to life. Nevertheless, there is a problem when we are so taken by a specific worldview, so enamored of it, that we elevate it into infinite status, making a god of it. We then walk through life with a mental grid into which we try to fit all people and all new experiences, at the expense of recognizing the integrity and mystery of others. Our grid then becomes a verbal fence by which we close out others, until and unless they enter our gates and consent to our truths. In Buddhism this clinging to a worldview is called "greed for views." In Christianity it is called "fundamentalism."

I suspect that, in certain moments of our lives, all of us are fundamentalists—even the most creative among us, even the poets. When poets struggle to compose a poem and then finally complete it, there is an impulse within them to rest in complete satisfaction, as if creation has come to an end. For a moment, they feel like God on the seventh day, and they've spoken their last word. But then they realize, as did God, that life goes on, bringing with it new experiences, requiring new responses, to which old patterns of thought are not entirely relevant. They discover that there is a mystery to life, a fluidity and creativity that cannot be captured by mental grids or even perfect poems. In Buddhism this fluidity is called "impermanence." In Christianity it is called "the continuing creation." Fundamentalism is a revolt against both. One of its deepest impulses is to freeze time.

When we fall into fundamentalism, we are never completely given to "the Illusion of Having a Perfect Set of Beliefs" that we hold on to. At one level, we are clinging to a mental grid of one sort or another that provides us with a sense of security and comfort. And yet at another and deeper level, we are dimly aware of an Open Space, beyond all mental grids, that supports us with sighs too deep for words. This Open Space is God. A central challenge in life is to learn to be still more trustful of this Open Space even as we appreciate, but do not cling to, the mental grids that help us make sense of the world.

There are many ways to die into this deeper trust. Usually the very circumstances of our lives require the dying. Something happens— we lose our jobs, we are shocked by a tragedy, we fall in love—and we find ourselves needing to let go of old ways of seeing things. Here life becomes our teacher. We die to our grids and, with God's help, arise to greater trust.

Another way to die into the trust is to spend some time each day in inner quietness, in mindful listening, in prayer. In so doing we gain a small bit of freedom from our mental grids, because we are quietly resting in the Open Space itself. Gradually, we begin to realize that Truth is always more than our concept of truth, that God is always more than our concept of God. This is not because God is so far away, but rather because God is so close, so intimate. Our mental grids often blind us to this closeness by reducing God to a mental construct, an object of belief, that resides in our heads. Silence helps unveil a deeper Truth. It is that God is within us—as a Holy Spirit— whose language is silence itself, who prays within us with sighs too deep for words.

With silence as our teacher, there can well up within us a sense of inner quietness, of prayerfulness, that is part of our daily life. We are better able to listen to other people on their own terms, cognizant that they need not enter God's pastures through our verbal gates. In this listening lies inner spaciousness, true freedom. It is a freedom to let God be God, to let others be themselves, and to let our own hearts grow toward what we are created to be: vessels of divine love.

In order to illustrate this listening, I turn to another image borrowed from poetry, which involves a re-imagining of the story of Adam and Eve and a resurrection of Eve's reputation. It is from a poem called "Eve: Night Thoughts," by Judson Jerome.[6] Let us revisit Adam and Eve in the Garden and give Eve appropriate recognition as a spiritual teacher.

Eve's Lesson to Adam

Eve was irritated. It was bad enough when Adam brought fire into the cave, almost incinerating their few possessions. After that he spent untold months chiseling rocks in order to invent the wheel. And then he tried to tame all the animals, bringing dogs into their home. His mind was so frenetic, so controlling. He seemed unable to sit still, to relax, to let things be.

Now something even worse was happening. He had decided to start naming everything. It was as if he was trying to build a verbal fence around the whole of life and even her. He wanted to tame the whole of creation with his categories.

So that night, while he was asleep, she came up with an idea. She decided that the next morning she would use words in an unusual way in order to help free Adam from his addiction to words and to verbal fences. It was Eve, then, who invented parodoxical language.

Who gave her this idea? She knew that some in the future would say "the devil." They would say that "truth" is a property of words and names, of creeds and dogmas, of prose and straightforward language. They would have no sense for metaphorical language and paradox and poetry. For Adam's sake, she was willing to face this.

Eve also knew that her critics would have no sense that there is a world beyond words: a world of birds and bugs and plants and women. She knew that her future critics would not realize that the sheer presence of creatures and of God is itself a kind of revelation, a kind of unveiling, though not a linguistic one. They would think that truth belongs only to words and not to the sheer presence of things as they are.

Still, Eve was confident. She knew that the devil was not her muse, but that instead God was. After all, God, too, liked to look at things without naming them. After laboring for six days, God had rested on the seventh, beholding her and her husband and the whole of creation in quiet joy. On that day—the first Sabbath—God wasn't giving commandments or using names. He was just watching the plants and animals, listening to their sounds and silences, in quiet joy. He was attending to the world beyond words.

Often Eve would enjoy this kind of consciousness with God as she walked through the fields and gardens. Sometimes she would look at Adam and appreciate him in the same way, not as something to be named and mentally enframed, but simply as a man she loved. She did indeed "observe the Sabbath" in these and other ways. Thus, she wanted Adam, too, to experience the spontaneous and preverbal presence of birds and plants and bugs and women, as they existed in their sheer is-ness, before being named. So that morning, upon waking, she uttered the first paradox ever spoken by a human being. "God is not really God," she said, "and I am not really Eve."

At first Adam was confused. He took her paradox as a contradiction. He thought that Eve was denying God's existence and even her own. But then he realized what she really meant. He saw that the beautifully intuitive woman lying next to him was not reducible to his name for her and that the Holy One who had created him was equally irreducible. In a flash of insight, he too discovered the world beyond words.

For days thereafter, Adam and Eve walked in silence, beholding the creation in sabbath consciousness. They felt close to each other and close to God. It was only after Adam learned to rest and be at home in silence that Eve then spoke to him, sharing an additional insight. "Now I need to tell you something, Adam. We can start talking to each other again, and we can even start naming things. It's fine to name things, just so our names don't become verbal fences, and just so, even as we name them, you see that they are more than your names. Sabbath consciousness is not limited to silence. It can be an underpinning for the world of sound."

With Eve's guidance, then, Adam slowly learned the art of gentle naming: that is, naming things without trying to control them. For several months they walked in the garden and began to use many names, although in a much softer and kinder way. They knew that dogs were more than "dogs" and bugs more than "bugs." They felt at home in silence and in sound, neither to the exclusion of the other.

It was at this point that Adam asked Eve a very important question: "And what shall we call our awareness of things as they exist in their own right, prior to our even naming them? What shall we call our sabbath consciousness?" Eve responded straightforwardly and clearly: "Let's call it prayer."

My image is a variation on Judson Jerome's "Eve: Night Thoughts." If you read Jerome's poem, you will see that my Eve is more sympathetic than his. Jerome has Eve inventing the lie; I have Eve inventing paradox. Jerome has Eve filled with resentment; I have her filled with loving irritation.

Still, I am indebted to Jerome's poem, not only for an image that serves as a springboard for my parable, but also for one very simple and important point. It is that our words and names can easily become verbal fences to which we cling almost as if they were gods and by which we then try to enframe the world at the expense of being open to its preverbal yet palpable presences. As a Christian, I know this sin from the inside. We Christians place a great deal of emphasis on words and creeds. It is no accident that, along with Jews and Muslims, we are known as "people of the Book." Our reliance not simply on oral speech but also on the printed word leads us to think that all valuable knowing is verbal knowing and with a tendency to enframe the whole of the world, and even God, in our theological grids. There is a good bit of Adam in all of us.

In addition, however, there is a bit of Eve. Even as we are tempted to enframe God and the world within our verbal grids, we are dimly aware that other people, plants and animals, trees and stars transcend our theological grids because they have is-ness in their own right. This "dim awareness" is what I mean by "sabbath consciousness" or "prayer."

The Wisdom of Silence

In Christianity there are many kinds of prayer. The well-known evangelical author Richard Foster has written a book in which he presents twenty-one types of prayer that are part of the Christian heritage. They range from "the prayer of adoration" through "petitionary prayer" to "healing prayer" and "the prayer of tears." Many, but not all, forms of Christian prayer use language, spoken inwardly or out loud. Much Christian prayer is verbal prayer.

Nevertheless, at least one form of Christian prayer is not verbal at all. Foster calls it "contemplative prayer," following the Christian tradition. In Foster's words, "Contemplative prayer is the one discipline that can free us from our addiction to words."[7]

In Christianity, *contemplation* means almost exactly the opposite of what it means in popular culture. In popular culture, contemplation implies a mental act of mulling over images and ideas, of thinking about things in a serious and earnest way, of reflecting on matters of import. In the Christian tradition, by contrast, contemplation means the opposite. It refers to a quiet and gentle listening in which words drop away and we listen to what is present.

The question at issue is, To what can we listen in such prayer? Here we will follow the lead of Russian Orthodox bishop Kallistos Ware. According to Ware, Orthodox Christianity offers two answers to this question, indicative of two different types of wordless, contemplative prayer.

On the one hand, we can listen to God. Ware calls this "the contemplation of God."[8] This kind of prayer would be analogous to Adam and Eve's feeling the presence of their creator without using names. In such listening, the creator is not exactly an external power, but more a pervasive and indwelling Beloved. The aim of this prayer is union with God.

On the other hand, we can listen to other people, other creatures, inner feelings, and events. Ware calls this "the contemplation of nature."[9] In this case we are inwardly drawn, not exactly to union with God, but rather to communion with the world. In terms of the parable offered above, it would be feeling the presence of other beings in a spirit of sabbath consciousness. It would be "observing the Sabbath."

Moreover, as Ware explains, there are two aspects to this sabbath consciousness, or contemplation of nature. The first might be called sacramental awareness, since it involves attending to some finite object—another person, a plant or animal, an inner feeling, an outer circumstance—as if it were a sacrament, a visible sign of an invisible grace. If, for example, Adam gazes into the eyes of Eve, beholding his beloved in her sheer presence, he may at the same time behold the presence of the divine Beloved, of God, in and through her eyes. Her eyes then become not only a gateway to her own soul but also a gateway to the divine Soul. Eve becomes a sacrament for Adam, a visible sign of an invisible grace.

In addition, however, she also becomes, for him, more fully herself. As he gazes into her eyes, he sees Eve in her own uniqueness, her own particularity, her own finitude. This is the kind of goodness that God saw on the seventh day. As God gazed at creation in wordless wonder, God was not just seeing Godself; God was seeing the creation, filled as it was with a goodness of its own. Adam sees this goodness when he looks at Eve. Ware calls this a perception of "suchness."

Ware makes clear that this way of perceiving can be applied to any living being, not just to human beings. In his words, "We are to see each stone, each leaf, each blade of grass, each frog, each human face, for what it truly is, in all the distinctness and intensity of its specific being. As the prophet Zechariah warns us, we are not to 'despise the day of small things.'"[10] My suggestion is that, as we see each stone and leaf and blade of grass in its individuality and uniqueness, we are seeing it as God sees it.

Let me summarize, then. In Christianity, *contemplative prayer* can refer both to a "contemplation of God" and a "contemplation of nature." As a contemplation of God, this kind of prayer involves a loss of self and an absorption in the Beloved. As a contemplation of nature it involves an appreciation of other living beings, events, and persons as beloveds through whom the Beloved is discovered and also an appreciation of other living beings as ends in themselves, in their suchness. It is on the latter dimension of the contemplation of nature that I focus in the closing of this chapter. I am interested in prayer as an awareness of suchness.

The Value of Meditation

How can we uncover our own capacities for a contemplation of nature? How can we grow in our capacity for appreciating the sheer is-ness, the suchness, of stones, leaves, blades of grass, and other human beings?

My own experience suggests that one of the most practical ways to enter into this form of prayer is through silent meditation.[11] By silent meditation I do not mean guided meditation, in which we imagine words or visualize scenes in our minds and then follow them. Nor do I mean meditation aimed at cultivating particular states of consciousness such as bliss or pleasure or even peace of mind. Rather, I mean meditation in which our sole aim, if it can be called an aim at all, is to relax into the present moment, let go of all distractions, and simply be aware, or mindful, of what is happening as it is happening.

If "what is happening" is that we are anxious, then our mindful awareness is to be aware of this anxiety. If "what is happening" is that the telephone is ringing, then our mindful awareness is to be aware of the ringing. If "what is happening" is that there is a pain in our knee, then our mindful awareness is to be aware of that pain. Two qualities inform this spacious awareness: attention and relaxation. These two qualities, taken together, are what Buddhists call "mindfulness" and what Christians call "the contemplation of nature."

In my own experience, one of the most helpful methods for uncovering our capacity for such mindfulness is seated meditation in Zen style, where for twenty or thirty minutes each morning, before the day begins, you sit quietly on the floor or in a chair with a straight back, breathing through your abdomen and following your breathing, without moving. The very act of not moving, even when you feel like it, involves a letting go of the need to always change things, to modify reality to suit your ego needs. Even if there is a pain in your knee, or someone enters the room, you do not move. And the act of breathing through your stomach allows you to enter more deeply into the natural and relaxed rhythms of breathing itself. The discipline of doing this every morning has helped me and many others to recover our capacity for patience, for deep listening, for mindfulness, which we can then bring into everyday life.

I am part of an ongoing meditation group, called Journey into Silence, that is committed to this daily practice at home and that meets once a week, for an hour, to sit together. Some of us are Christian, some Buddhist, and some none-of-the-above. We never discuss theology, but we are jointly committed to silence, however understood, as a path through which we find God. My participation in this group forms a kind of anchor in my life, perpetually reminding me that the world around me and within me is a world beyond words, full of suchness, and that the God to whom I seek to entrust my heart finds me in my openness to this world.

Of course, Zen meditation is not for everybody. One can find silence through yoga, walks in the woods, drawing, and even poetry, when the poetry takes one beyond words. What is for everybody, each in his or her own way, is some opportunity each day to take a sabbath from busyness, from changing things, from the noisiness of consumer culture, in order to listen deeply and richly to the stone, the leaf, the blade of grass, the frog, and the face. This deep listening, filled with silence, is an act of lying gently in the waters of divine love, even if those waters are not named or recognized. More important than the naming is the letting go into mindful awareness, which is itself a letting go into love.

CHAPTER FIVE

Trust in Open Space
Spirituality as Faith in God

There's a wideness in God's mercy
like the wideness of the sea.

Frederick W. Faber (1854)

...there are fields and fields,
and fields aplenty, more and more
space than is needed, ample space
for any kind of sin to be laid down,
disassembled, swallowed away, lost,
absorbed, forgotten, transformed,
if one should only ask
for such a favor.

Pattiann Rogers[1]

It is true that sin is the cause of all this pain, but all will
be well, and every kind of thing will be well.

Julian of Norwich[2]

Sometimes, if something terrible has happened in our lives, it can help to follow the advice of Walt Whitman. It can help to go outside on a clear night and gaze into the dark and starlit sky in perfect silence.

The sky and its stars can be a holy icon, an enfolding womb in which we feel small but included in a greater wholeness. The greater wholeness is God, the Open Space. The moist night air, which gives freedom and freshness to our souls, is God's Breathing.

121

We experience this Breathing in two ways. First, we experience it through the healing grace of the sky itself, which reminds us that there is something more to the universe, much more, than is contained in our suffering, no matter how intense it might be. Here, the sky functions as a stained glass window through which divine light shines: a dark light, to be sure, but a holy light as well.

Second, we experience the Breathing through our own internal amazement and wonder at the spectacle of the sky, through our delight in the beauty of its thousand points of light. In our amazement God breathes as deeply as the sky itself. Complementing this amazement, there can also emerge an additional and more subtle feeling: a sense of opening out into the night sky and trusting the mysterious presence, the dark mystery, that shines through it. This opening out into trust is what I mean by "faith" in this chapter. Faith is a trustful letting go, in which we open out into the divine mystery and feel included in a larger whole. It is trust in Open Space.

Faith has a healing effect in our lives, and it can get us through almost any difficulty. But it does not do so by changing the objective situation. Rather, it does so by giving us the inner resources to deal with a bad situation, no matter how horrible it might be. Let us be honest. The dark and starlit sky does not and cannot eliminate the terrible happening that makes us sad. The larger whole—the Open Space—does not change the fact that our loved one has died, our friend has deserted us, we have sinned terribly, the end has come. Nothing can reverse the past, not even God.

God and Eric Falling

For the sake of illustration, consider Eric Morris. On October 13, 1994, he was pushed out of the upper story window of an apartment in the Ida B. Wells Housing Project of Chicago. His killers were two boys, one ten and one eleven, who were punishing him for not helping them steal candy. Eric was five years old.

For my part, I hope that Eric continues to live in some state of life-after-death, growing into whatever wholeness is possible for him. I hope the same for the boys who pushed him, who did not know what they were doing, and for all living beings, including those who do know what they are doing when they commit horrible crimes. "May all being be happy," goes the Buddhist prayer. This seems to me a prayer worth praying.

Nevertheless, I am haunted by the image of Eric falling. It seems to me that there is nothing that can happen, not even heavenly rehabilitation, that can reverse this horrible happening. Once something has happened like this, it cannot un-happen.

Moreover, when that something is happening, it can be obscenely horrifying. I have a young son myself. I know how Matthew feels when he wakes up from a nightmare. He feels out of control and alone, as if his world is coming to an end. Eric must have experienced a similar kind of terror, except that he *was* out of control and his world *was* coming to an end. There was no father to assure him that everything was all right. There were no hands to catch him. Not even God's.

Where was God when Eric fell? We cannot avoid the question.

Option 1: God was in the sky watching Eric. This is the way many people picture God. They use the word *God* to refer to a personal being, residing off the planet, who created the world a long time ago and who intervenes from time to time, but who did not intervene in Eric's case. For them, God is an all-powerful father who loves us deeply and can do anything he wants but who does not prevent suffering. As these people see it, God could have saved Eric, if not by direct intervention, then by creating a world in which small boys were better protected. But he had his reasons for not saving Eric and for creating this kind of world. "God wants us to be free," they say, "and Eric's falling is the price of freedom gone astray."

Option 2: God was not in the sky at all, and God is not a personal being either. Rather, God is the energy of the universe itself, which is indifferent to the plight of individuals and which unfolds in ways both terrible and beautiful, both hateful and compassionate. This is the way some others picture God. Many among them are alienated by the image of a cosmic father, because he seems too condemning, too authoritarian, and too male. For them, the word *God* does not name a being among beings, not even a supreme being, but rather the energy and power of the universe itself. This means that whatever happens in our universe—including the choice that Eric's friends made to push him out the window and Eric's falling itself—is the very activity of God. These happenings are God godding.

Option 3: God is an Opened Heart within which the universe unfolds, sharing in the joys and sufferings of each creature and luring each creature toward whatever wholeness is possible for it in the situation at hand, but necessarily limited by the decisions and actions— the creativity—of the creatures.

In this book I am recommending the third option, which is that of process theology. I think it helps us see how God shared in the suffering and terror of Eric as he fell, but it also explains why God did not prevent the boys from pushing Eric out the window in the first place and nevertheless shows that God can help heal tragedy, bringing resurrection out of death. In the next chapter I will outline the worldview of process theology in terms of which this option makes sense.

But for now let us note that this third option invites attention to two of the nine ways of being breathed by God that this book highlights: courage in suffering and trust in Open Space.

Courage in Suffering

By "courage in suffering" I mean two things. First, I mean being present to other people who are suffering and thus sharing in their pain, even though we might not be able to repair their situation. This kind of presence can also be felt in relation to other living beings— animals, for example. If we have courage in suffering, we can be with them in their time of horror, just as God is with them in their time of horror. Another name for this "being present to others" is empathy: feeling the feelings of others as they feel them. It is one type of loving-kindness, but it deserves a special treatment in its own right because it is so important in life.

In the second place, by "courage in suffering" I mean a capacity to endure our own suffering, without hiding or running away, until it can run its course in our lives. In this regard I sometimes think of Eric's mother and the courage she must have had to find, within herself, to deal with the loss of her beloved son. My suggestion is that we are breathed by God when we exhibit this kind of courage in our own losses and heartbreaks. We must live with our own suffering and ride out our own pain until it runs out. This riding out of pain is one of the deepest ways we can dwell with God.

If we are to have this courage, it can help if it is undergirded by still another way of being breathed by God. I call it "faith in God" or "trust in Open Space." In what follows I offer two examples of what I mean by faith and then offer a definition.

Paul's Widening into Faith

The first comes from the New Testament and is a story that Christians know well. As a man named Saul journeyed to Damascus, something remarkable and strange happened to him. He was blinded by a heavenly light, fell to the ground, and heard the voice of Jesus saying, "Saul, Saul, why do you persecute me?" The experience shook his soul to the core. As a Pharisee with fundamentalist leanings, he had been persecuting fellow Jews who had joined the Nazarene sect. Now he was stopped in his tracks. The Nazarene himself, returned from the dead, challenged him with a fierce yet tender love.

Then, over the next few days, something equally remarkable occurred. With the help of a spiritual companion named Ananias, Saul's heart was opened. He changed his name to Paul and became a friend to the very people whom he had been persecuting. He accepted their forgiveness and came to see that God was loving, much more loving than he had ever imagined. In short: something went wide in him.

This process of "going wide" is what I mean by faith. Faith is an interior movement of the soul, invisible to outsiders, in which the heart opens out into the Open Space and the Open Space wells up in the heart. Always this "going wide" involves a trustful letting go of icons that have become idols, of congealings that have become too solid.

In Paul's case, the "congealings" were the good but finite teachings of Pharisaic Judaism and the pride he had in conforming to them. They had been, for him, sacraments, until he clung to them too fiercely. The "trustful letting go" involved a relinquishment of religious convictions to which he was inordinately attached. These included the convictions that his own religion—the way of the Pharisees—had complete truth, that the gentle Nazarenes were evil, and that the Nazarene himself was a false messiah. He had a great deal invested in these convictions, so the letting go was not easy. It was only through a special revelation, from the Nazarene himself, that the letting go could occur.

Of course, Paul's own capacities for faith—for trustful letting go—were always finite. His growth into wideness, into a full understanding of what he discovered on the road to Damascus, was never complete. We know from his letters that he had to adapt to new situations again and again and that, in the process, he was further transformed by the love that befell him, and felled him, on the road to Damascus. Sometimes we wish he had been transformed a bit more. We lament some of his attitudes toward people who displeased him: the Jews who chose not to follow him, the Nazarenes with alternate teachings, the "fornicators" and "liars." He seems not to have been as gentle or forgiving as was the Nazarene.

Indeed, we suspect that he was never quite cured of the fundamentalism that plagued his earlier life. After his conversion, as before, he had a tendency to think that he was "right" about most things and others "wrong." He seems to have clung too tightly to his own opinions, at the expense of being open to that Mystery that can always be trusted but never clung to.

And yet we are not really different from him. In our lives, too, there are moments when we are called to grow beyond a fundamentalist outlook into which we have fallen, to grow into a deeper and less clinging form of trust, and to allow our hearts to widen. This process is often called "spiritual growth."

My proposal is that we are beckoned into this kind of growth at each moment of our lives, that the beckoning occurs within us at levels too deep for words, that the beckoning comes from God and is God, and that we are embraced by the Holy, even when we do not respond to the beckoning. In other words, even though we are called to holiness, we are embraced by God just as we are, holy or not. As Paul liked to put it, we are saved, not by our works, or even by our growth, but by grace through faith.

What is it like to experience grace through faith? Paul's way was through the resurrected Jesus. Mine is too. And yet there are other, complementary paths. Not only messiahs but also trembling tree branches can reveal the grace at the heart of things. Consider, then, a second example of faith.

Seeing through the Swirling

I borrow the image from a poem called "A Gap in the Cedar" by Roy Scheele.[3] The poem begins with the image of a man standing in a room, looking out a window, on a winter's day. The man seems solemn and sad, as if someone he loves has died. He is gazing at the trees and snow when something very subtle strikes his eye. It is the trembling of a branch from a cedar tree.

> I saw this much from the window:
> the branch spring lightened into place
> with a lithe shudder of snow.

He surmises that the branch sprang back into place because a bird had been on it and had just flown away. But he doesn't know, or even need to know, what kind of bird it was.

> Whatever bird had been there,
> chickadee or sparrow,
> had so vanished into air,
> resilient, beyond recall,

it had to be taken on faith
to be taken at all.

What he does know, however, is that as he sees the branch spring into place, something goes wide in his heart. He sees something and knows something that momentarily dispels the sadness of the moment.

In the moment it took the tree
to recover that trembling
something went wide in me—
there was a rush of wings,
the air beaten dim with snow,
and then I saw through the swirling.

And thus the poem ends. Something went wide in this man, and he saw through the swirling.

What did he see? The poem doesn't tell us. But the title of the poem, "A Gap in the Cedar," gives us a hint. He saw a clearing, a gap, an open space, between the branches of the cedar tree. And the very seeing of this open space widened his heart, helping him to get through this day and perhaps many days thereafter. He began the process of healing from his grief by seeing the gap in the cedar.

My suggestion is that the "gap in the cedar" that this man saw, in his way and his time, was the very God "in whom we live and move and have our being," as discovered by Paul. And my suggestion is that the "seeing through the swirling" that briefly dispelled his sadness and opened up a larger horizon of hope was the very "faith" that saved Paul too. He, too, was saved by grace through faith. He, too, was saved by trust.

The purpose of "seeing though the swirling" in a moment of awakening is to contribute to everyday life. If we cling to an awakening experience, such as that had by the man in the poem, we are missing the point. The point of authentic living is to live in a spirit of "trustful letting go" in each moment of our lives, in ways that are wise, compassionate, and free. In this life of "trustful letting go," we are obedient to the call of each moment. We laugh when it is time to laugh; we cry when it is time to cry; we eat when it is time to eat; we sleep when it is time to sleep. Each moment, and every moment, is a moment in which the Infinite becomes the finite, in which the Wideness of the Open Space becomes a wideness in our own hearts. All that is necessary for this to occur is that we be able to let go, day by day and moment by moment. All that is necessary is faith.

Faith as Trust in Open Space

What, then, is faith? It is trust in Open Space. I use the word *trust* as a substitute for faith, because the word *faith* sometimes suggests intellectual assent to verbal creeds. When I say "faith," I do not mean intellectual assent to phrases such as "God exists" or "There is a sacred dimension to reality" or "The ultimate Truth is Love." This kind of assent is better called "belief in good ideas" or "the holding of worthy convictions." Such belief can contribute to faith and be supported by faith, but it is not identical to faith.

For example, when I was a Christian fundamentalist, I had lots of belief but not much faith. I clung ferociously to a verbal fence made of words and doctrines, which I called Christianity. But I did not trust that God might lie outside the confines of my fence. If God is a pasture for gazelles, full of nourishing grace, and if we humans are the gazelles grazing in this green pasture, then I was trying to get all the gazelles into my pen. I was holding up a sign that said "Only those who enter this pen can be saved." I did not trust in open space.

Additionally, I was pretty sure that God was located in my pen, at the expense of being present in other locations. I use the phrase "Open Space" as an alternative to "God" in this book because the word "God" too easily suggests a male deity residing off the planet, onto which we can grasp or cling. When I say "God," I do not mean something we can grasp in this way. By "God" I mean a vast and mysterious Clearing—a sky-like Mind—in which we live and move and have our being. God is the Wideness, the Spacious Awareness, by which our own inner lives are widened when something goes wide in our hearts.

My thesis, then, is that the defining characteristics of faith in God are "trustful letting go" and "going wide." These are not observable acts or deeds. They are interior movements of the soul. When they are undergone in a continuous way, they become habits of the heart, as much unconscious as conscious. They are what happens in us when, as Paul puts it, the eyes of our heart are enlightened.

The Wisdom of Faith

This enlightenment—this wisdom of faith—is not a matter of hearing some words and understanding their meanings. It is not philosophical or discursive wisdom. It is not theology. Rather, it is more direct and intuitive, like listening to music. When we listen to music, we know the music by feeling it. It fills our souls and widens our hearts. Often, it gladdens us. Analogously, when we dwell in faith, we know God by feeling God. God fills our souls and widens our hearts. In this gladdening and widening, there is deep knowing. There is the wisdom of faith.

What, then, is intuitively known in the life of trustful letting go? What is the wisdom of faith? Any answer to this question will involve words and ideas, and hence a reversion to a more verbalized dimension of human life. This does not mean that the knowing itself is verbal. It simply means that a discussion of what we know is verbal. Here, then, is what I think we know. I think we know that

- There is a deep mystery in life—something more—and it is good
- There is a grace sufficient to each moment
- There is a wideness in God's mercy
- All will be well

If the wisdom of faith is akin to the wisdom of listening to music, then these four insights are, as it were, what we know when we listen to the music. They are the musical score for the music of faith. In some moments we can know more of one than the other, but all four represent the fullness of faith. In what follows I comment on each.

There Is Something More

First, we know that there is something more to life, much more, than our own finite experience—including its pains and sorrows—can ever quite understand. I borrow from the phrase from Lillah McCarthy. She was a British actress and theater manager who worked closely with the playwright George Bernard Shaw and whose husband deserted her. In her time of distress, she went to Shaw for comfort and fell into a moment of faith.

> I was shivering. Shaw sat very still. The fire brought me warmth…How long we sat there I do not know, but presently I found myself walking with dragging steps with Shaw beside me…up and down Adelphi Terrace. The weight upon me grew a little lighter and released the tears which would never come before…He let me cry. Presently I heard a voice in which all the gentleness and tenderness of the world was speaking. It said: "Look up, dear, look up to the heavens. There is more in life than this. There is much more."[4]

What did she see when she gazed into the sky? What did Shaw mean by the "much more" in life? Bishop Kallistos Ware, from whom I borrow this story, offers the following interpretation:

Whatever his own faith in God or lack of it, Shaw points here to something that is fundamental to the spiritual Way. He did not offer smooth words of consolation to Lillah McCarthy, or pretend that her pain would be easy to bear. What he did was more perceptive. He told her to look out for a moment from herself, from her personal tragedy, and to see the world in its objectivity, to sense its wonder and variety, its "thusness." And his advice applies to all of us. However oppressed by my own or others' anguish, I am not to forget that there is more in the world than this. There is much more.[5]

Ware's interpretation is immensely insightful. So often we are healed by recognizing that there is an objective world beyond us that has a life of its own quite apart from our suffering. Part of the "something more" is the objective world itself.

But I like to think that the "something more" is also that ultimate horizon—that wide open space—within which the whole of the universe resides. My name for this moreness, of course, is God. For me, God is the encircling presence, shining through a dark and starlit sky, within which all things are small but included: the stars and planets, the hills and rivers, the joys and sorrows. Faith, then, is making contact with God by means of trust. It is a *trustful letting go, in which something goes wide in our hearts, and we see into the Open Space,* gaining perspective on our lives.

For example, in the case of Lillah McCarthy, such "trustful letting go and going wide" occurred when she cried. Prior to this moment, she was like many of us when we suffer deeply. She was suffering deeply, and she was inwardly attached to her sadness. There was a weight upon her soul. Her soul was contracted. This weight, this inner contraction, was then lifted with the help of Shaw's kind words and healing presence: "The weight upon me grew a little lighter and released the tears which would never come before…He let me cry." In the crying itself, there was then a "trustful letting go and going wide." Her crying was a prayer of lamentation and thus a "no" to the fact that her husband had left her. But it was also a "yes" to the mystery of life. At this moment, she fell into faith, which is a little like falling in love. Deep tears, no less than deep laughter, can be ways of opening into the Open Space.

"Trustful letting go and going wide" are also what happened when, after crying, she looked into the heavens and realized the truth of what Shaw was saying: "There is more to life than this. There is much more." Here, too, Shaw was a sacramental presence. His words were a means by which the light of heaven shined into her heart, melting chilly confines of self-containment. Not only tears, but very good friends who have the capacity for silence and deep listening can be holy icons. But the night sky was itself also a sacramental presence: a means by which divine light shined into her life.

When she gazed into the night sky, she saw the Open Space. This mysterious moreness was not simply an idea she grasped with her mind. It was not a puzzle to be solved. Rather, it was a felt presence, a divine Mystery. As she opened out into this Mystery, her sadness assumed its place in the larger scheme of things. She saw the Mystery as an open space, an ample space, that could absorb and transform even the most painful of sins and sufferings. And so it was and still is. The Mystery of life is not something to which we can cling. It is an Open Space into which we can widen when something goes wide in our hearts.

There Is a Grace Sufficient to Each Moment

If the first thing we know in faith is that there is "something more" in life, the second thing we know is that there is a grace sufficient to each moment. By "grace" I mean fresh possibilities for responding to the situation at hand, whatever that situation, and fresh energy for actualizing those possibilities. To dwell in faith is to trust that, whatever happens, fresh possibilities will be available for responding in healing and whole-making ways to what happens, and it is to trust that we ourselves will have the strength to actualize them, no matter how weary we feel.

These fresh possibilities are not all-powerful. They are simply the best for the situation at hand. They are fresh possibilities for hope in times of despair, for laughter in times of sadness, for courage in times of fear, for relaxation in times of weariness. To trust in God is to trust in the availability of these possibilities. It is trust that there is a grace sufficient to each moment.

Here, of course, a profound question emerges. Are there not some times in a person's life when there is not grace sufficient to the moment, when the only possible grace for a given moment is sadness, or confusion, or sheer terror? Recall Eric Morris. What grace was sufficient to his moment of falling from the building?

To this question I can only respond as did Whitehead: that one of the deepest gifts we can receive from God in some circumstances of our lives is unconsciousness or sleep. For my part, I think the grace sufficient to Eric's life, in his moment of falling, was itself a falling into unconsciousness. And I trust that his terror, and his falling into unconsciousness, was itself shared by God.

There Is a Wideness in God's Mercy

The third thing we know in faith, then, is that there is a wideness in God's mercy. In human life there are at least three contexts in which we need this wideness: sin, suffering, and foolishness.

The Christian tradition has stressed the relevance of the sin and suffering. We Christians have taken the wideness of Jesus' heart, as he lay dying on the cross, as expressive of a wideness in the very Heart of the universe. Just as Jesus absorbed the sorrows of those around him, sharing in their suffering, so God absorbs the sorrows of the world, sharing in them. And just as Jesus took on the sins of the world, forgiving those who knew not what they were doing in killing him, so God takes on the sins of the world, forgiving those who do not understand what they are doing.

The poet Pattian Rogers expresses the latter wisdom when she says that in our universe

...there are fields and fields,
and fields aplenty, more and more
space than is needed, ample space
for any kind of sin to be laid down,
disassembled, swallowed away, lost,
absorbed, forgotten, transformed,
if one should only ask
for such a favor.[6]

In Jesus' death on the cross, he reveals that deeply plentiful Field in which these "fields aplenty" reside. It is God as the Open Space, the Ample Space, the Merciful Gap in the Cedar.

Equally important, however, is the intuitive recognition that the Ample Space absorbs foolishness and imperfection. Some people in our world take themselves far too seriously and expect themselves to be perfect in ways that are inhumane and unhuman. In the age of consumerism, this "perfection" sometimes amounts to being attractive, affluent, and accomplished. People who fall short of these goals then feel inferior and imperfect. They feel that they have not lived up to the expectations of society, that they do not "measure up," that they are "unsuccessful."

Needless to say, these perfections are themselves imperfect. They are false substitutes for the deeper perfections of wisdom, compassion, and freedom. The world needs more "perfectionists" who seek wisdom, compassion, and freedom in their lives, and fewer who seek appearance, affluence, and goal-driven achievement. But perfectionism of any variety can take its toll. Some of the saddest people in the world are those who are deeply committed to the best of ideals in all the wrong ways. Seeking to be perfectly wise, compassionate, and free, they become obsessive in their quests for purity and thus incapable of accepting their own humanity. They cannot laugh at themselves or laugh with others, because they are too busy trying to be perfect. Thus, part of the deeper wisdom of faith lies in its intuitive recognition that, in many contexts, it is all right to be imperfect. All right to be un-whole. All right to be un-integrated. All right to be human. The Open Space is an ample space that can include even our humanity.

This, I think, is what Paul meant when he said that we are saved by grace through faith. He meant that we are saved, not by becoming perfect, but by knowing that we are loved even amid our imperfections. We do not have to be perfect to be loved. We are loved just as we are.

All Will Be Well

The fourth thing we know in faith is that, in some mysterious way that we can never completely understand this side of death, "all will be well and every kind of thing will be well."[7] The words belong to Julian of Norwich, the anchoress who lived in solitude in Norwich, England, in the late fourteenth century. This revelation of wellness occurred in one of sixteen "showings" she received from God.

The intuition of ultimate wellness, of ultimate safety and joy, is a complement to the Buddhist prayer: May all beings be happy. It is an intuition that, in the last analysis, and in ways we cannot understand, all beings will be happy, and this despite two contrary realities.

The first reality is that, in the present, many beings are terribly unhappy. Julian thought that most unhappiness was due to sin. I am not so sure. I think a good bit is due to greed, hatred, and the confusion that we fall into, despite our own better selves, and some is due to pain that is foisted upon us, like the painful sensation of falling from a tall building, as in the case of Eric Morris. The intuition that all will be well must be honest about the reality of unhappiness in our world, not hiding from it by suggesting that all beings are already happy, if they but knew it. They are not already happy.

The second and contrary reality is evil itself. By evil I do not mean moral evil. I do not have in mind the cruelty that might lie in someone's heart that then might be expressed in a horrible act. Rather, I have in mind tragedy. I mean the reality of terrible suffering, such as that felt by Eric falling, and I mean the reality of missed potential, such as that which occurred with his death. From the perspective of process theology, these two realities—unnecessary suffering and a cutting off of potential—are the two kinds of evil we face in life, both of which coalesce in the suffering and then death of a small child.

My point, then, is that if we say "all will be well," our sense of eventual wellness cannot hide from, or even minimize, the reality of unhappiness and evil in the world. Even if all becomes well, it seems to me that there are some things that happen in our world, concerning which we must say, even in light of ultimate wellness, "Despite the wellness, things would have been better had it never occurred."

Nevertheless, in moments of deep faith, I think we know that all will be well. Process theology offers two images of wellness, both of which may capture what is known when we feel, deep within, that all will be well.

The first is that all happenings in the universe—including Eric and his falling—are remembered forevermore in the life of God and woven into a greater whole. This would be to say that the ultimate meaning of the universe does not lie in any particular finite being, not even Eric, but rather in the non-finite being, the opened heart, of the divine life as it retains and preserves all that happens with a tender care that nothing be forgotten. Put simply, Eric does not live on as a self-conscious being with a life of his own, but rather as a memory in the larger life of God.

The second image is, for me, more promising. It is the image of all finite beings, including Eric, living on in their individual journeys, even after death, until wholeness can be realized, as elicited by God's lure toward healing and wholeness. In the case of Eric, for example, this would mean that he himself continues to live, even after his death, such that he can experience that completeness that he lacked in his final moments. This completeness would not eliminate the fact that, all things considered, it would have been better had he not fallen in the first place. It is a completeness that becomes possible after the fact and despite the fact that the suffering ought not to have occurred.

In human life, most of us experience this completeness in moments when we are forgiven of our sins by others. Perhaps this kind of forgiveness is what Eric's young killers received afterward. I hope so.

To their dying day, they will always look back on what they did and wish that they had not done it. Even after death, they will look back and have this wish. Still, if they have been forgiven by those who loved Eric, and if they can forgive themselves, they will know a completeness that is unparalleled. There will be a restoration of broken relationships, a coming together in love.

Ultimately, of course, we are all those boys. And we are all Eric. We all undergo terrible sufferings that we wish we had not had to undergo, and we all inflict suffering on others that we wish we had not inflicted. Life on Earth involves disharmonies, broken relations, that need reconciliation, in this life and in the next.

What we know in faith is that, in the last analysis, this reconciliation will occur. The lion will lie down with the lamb, and the lamb with the lion. The killer with the victim, and the victim with the killer. In some moments of our lives, perhaps when we gaze deeply into a starlit sky, we feel this and know this. In our feeling and knowing, we are then free to be honest about our sins and to be healers in a broken world. We are free to live from the Center. We are saved by grace through faith.

CHAPTER SIX

Even the Stars Pray
A Cosmology for Centered Living

The LORD is my shepherd, I shall not want.
He makes me lie down in green pastures;
he leads me besides still waters;
he restores my soul.
He leads me in right paths
for his name's sake.
Even though I walk through the darkest valley,
I fear no evil;
for you are with me;
your rod and your staff—they comfort me.

Psalm 23:1–4

All things bright and beautiful,
All creatures great and small,
All things wise and wonderful,
The Lord God loves them all.

Cecil F. Alexander (1848)

Imagine that we are sheep grazing in green pastures and that the Lord truly is our shepherd. Suppose further that the Lord is not a particular deity residing off the planet, but rather an encircling presence, around the universe and within the universe, who seeks to guide all living beings into healing and wholeness, in this life or in the next. Each creature would then be a sheep, each with its wild and precious life. For example, each human being would be a sheep,

137

whether tall or short, young or old, happy or sad, kind or mean. But so would each sparrow and pine tree, each star and planet. Even spirits and ancestors would be sheep.

Thus, the pasture would be the universe itself, with its many dimensions, some visible and some invisible. There would be nothing outside the pasture except the Lord's encircling presence. The good news would be that the universe is enfolded within the invisible arms of a very good Shepherd, whose opened heart includes all things bright and beautiful, all creatures great and small, and also the bad and lost sheep, the ones who are despised, feared, and abandoned by the rest. The abused child would be part of the divine pasture, but so would the abusing parent, who knows not what he does.

Indeed, this good Shepherd might best be imagined in still more intimate terms. The Lord who is our shepherd might also be conceived as a Beloved in whose arms we lie, even if we feel alone and unlovable. After all, not many of us have intimate contact with shepherds. But all of us want to love and be loved. The good news would be that the heart of the universe is love and that we belong to its deepest embrace. Our need is to feel the whisper of our Beloved.

Imagine further that we can feel this whisper in many, many ways. I have discussed nine of them in this book: discernment, sacramental awareness, openness to healing, living-by-dying, trust in open space, deep listening, courage in suffering, creativity, and loving-kindness. I have suggested that we can experience our Beloved's breathing in the very grass beneath our feet, when we look at it in amazement and wonder; in our kindred sheep, when we treat them with loving-kindness; and in the stars above, when we gaze at them in holy awe, cognizant that we are part of a deeper cosmic adventure. I have proposed that the very purpose of life is to be breathed by our Beloved and thus dwell in communion with the stars, the grass, and the sheep.

If this is the case, then two questions emerge: What is the valley of the shadow of death? And what is the path of righteousness that can carry us through this valley?

The Valley of the Shadow of Death

I suggest that the valley of the shadow of death consists of two realities. It consists of (1) the terrible sufferings and losses we face as individuals and communities, which are often the worst not when they happen to us but when they happen to others whom we love.

And it consists of (2) the greeds, hatreds, and envies into which we fall, amid which we become our worst selves. If these two realities form the valley of the shadow of death, then the first is probably part of the human condition. There will always be tragedy and loss. That is why courage in suffering, loving-kindness, and faith are such important ways of being breathed by God. They help us live with suffering and loss without hiding or running away.

The second aspect of the valley seems more malleable, at least when the greed, hatred, and envy are nurtured by social conditions and cultural influences. In our time a dominant influence for greed and envy, if not also hatred, is the culture of consumerism. It tells us that money is our shepherd, that competition is our path, that a green pasture is but real estate. It leads us to treat our fellow sheep not as kindred creatures in a communion of subjects but as competitive consumers in a world of objects. It treats even the Lord as an absentee landowner, deaf to the prayers of all but the most prosperous of sheep. In relation to this cultural atmosphere and its overconsuming lifestyle, we do indeed need a path of righteousness.

The Path of Righteousness

And what is the path of righteousness? In this book I speak of it as "living from the Center" and "practicing the presence of God" and "living prayerfully." Along with other Christians, I think that this living is the Way that was revealed in Jesus, and this Way is itself the Truth and the Life. Wherever we see this Way, we see God in the world.

But along with Buddhists, I think that there are eighty-four thousand gates into this Way, none of them reducible to a single set of beliefs or a single religion. Whoever inhales the Breath of God in a single moment is entering a gate in that moment.

The question then becomes, And how can we live from the Center, how can we walk the path of righteousness, in a more consistent way? I suggest that the answer lies in three dimensions of our lives: our minds, our hearts, and our actions. When these three dimensions of our lives are enlivened by the spirit of God, we are walking the path of righteousness. To use Buddhist terminology, we embody "right thinking" and "right acting" and "right breathing."

In much of this book I have been dealing with the third dimension, right breathing, because it is too often neglected. Too often religiously interested people equate healthy living with the practical application of fervently held convictions. When religion is reduced to the first two dimensions—right thinking and right acting—three problems easily emerge: (1) fundamentalism, in which there is an overemphasis on right thinking; (2) burnout, in which there is an overemphasis on right acting; and (3) the will-to-mastery, in which we try to make the world "believe as we believe" or "act as we act" without regard for the independent needs of others. In order to avoid these three problems, our thinking and acting need to be animated by a source of healing energy that is more than any project we undertake with our wills or idea that we embrace with our minds. This source is God's Breathing. It widens the room of our hearts so that we can act creatively and wisely in the world.

Nevertheless, spirituality, or "right breathing," is not enough. We also need right thinking and right acting. My aim in this final chapter is to turn to the third of these three dimensions of healthy living. I want to say a word about the spirit of right thinking in the age of consumerism, to recommend a worldview—that of process theology—as one among several worldviews that offer a cosmology conducive to spiritual living, and to recommend a set of guidelines for right acting in the age of consumerism.

Right Thinking in the Age of Consumerism

I emphasized at the outset that there are many forms of right thinking. We can think rightly as Buddhists or Christians, Hindus or Muslims, Jews or Free Spirits. If we are open to Truth to the best of our lights, then we have entered the spirit of right thinking.

By right thinking, then, I mean two things. First, I mean the holding of worthy ideas such as "God is love" and "Healing is possible" and "All things are interconnected" and "Greed brings suffering." It seems to me that these ideas are more honest and more truthful than their opposites: "God is hatred" and "Healing is impossible" and "All things are isolated" and "Greed is a virtue." I think that Buddhists and Christians, Hindus and Muslims, Jews and Free Spirits can hold these ideas, all in their own ways.

Second, and equally important, I mean a certain way of holding these ideas such that, even as we hold them, we realize their limitations. More specifically, I mean holding these convictions with an inner sense that the words and concepts we use—even those that are most important to us—are like fingers pointing to the moon and not the moon itself. They are helpful pointers, but they are not the objects they represent. In short, "right thinking" involves a humble recognition of the limitations of words and concepts.

When such humility informs our thinking, our thinking becomes a form of prayer, even as it may be rational and analytical, creative and imaginative. At least, this is the case if by prayer we mean inner availability to God as Mystery. If our thinking is imbued with a spirit of humility, we are holding on to concepts firmly but lightly, because we realize that the Truth is more than our concept of truth. In this realization there is availability to the Mystery. There is prayer.

For most of us, of course, this firm-but-light way of holding on to concepts does not come easily. Precisely because our concepts give us a sense of grounding, we are tempted to cling to them as if they were absolutes. We say "God is Love" and then hold on to our own understanding of the phrase as if the phrase itself were God. We fall into what Buddhists call "greed for views." Right thinking involves freedom from mental greed, because it trusts in a Mystery that is more than the intellect.

This trust can be supported by a complementary recognition that there are many ways of knowing Truth besides knowing through ideas and words. These other ways of approaching Truth include musical knowing, in which we know things about life through sound and rhythm; empathic knowing, in which we know things about other people by feeling their feelings; and intuitive knowing, in which we know things about reality through wordless awakenings. Such alternative forms of knowing are important sources of truth, but they do not involve words and concepts. Right thinking, then, is only one form of knowing. This is why there is more to wisdom than right thinking. Some people who are wise do not think very well, and some people who think well are not very wise.

Equally important, right thinking sometimes involves, and even requires, questioning and doubt. Certainly, there are times in our lives when it is good to be clear about what we believe and to stick to those beliefs with fervor. It is good, for example, to believe that "rape and murder are wrong." But on other kinds of matters, particularly of a cosmological or theological kind, there is a place for questioning and doubt. When it comes to the nature of God, there is often more knowing in the honest agnostic, who knows that God, if God exists, is always more than anyone's concept of God, than in the fervent theist who says "I know God's nature" but who lacks humility in his knowing. Often there is more understanding in a person who asks the right questions but has no easy answers than in one who has all the answers but never asks the questions. Genuine doubt is a healthy companion, and perhaps a necessary companion, to healthy belief.

Why Worldviews Matter

Nevertheless, worldviews matter. By worldview I mean a "theology" or "philosophy" or "cosmology" that helps us make sense of our experiences and our world. If you are Christian, for example, your worldview will include the idea that there is a God whose deepest nature is love and whose love was revealed, but not exhausted, in a carpenter from Nazareth. If you are Buddhist, your worldview will include the idea that all living beings—even plants and animals—possess a potentiality for enlightenment called the Buddha-nature.

On the other hand, if you are committed to a more mechanistic understanding of the world, you may well believe that these ideas within Christianity and Buddhism are but figments of the human imagination, because there is no "God" or "Buddha-nature." Perhaps you believe that reality is reducible to matter-in-motion, that matter consists of atoms and molecules, that atoms and molecules are lifeless and inert, and that all things can be completely explained by their behavior. Whitehead, the founder of process philosophy, called this perspective "scientific materialism."[1]

Of course, most contemporary scientists are not scientific materialists. Many contemporary scientists do not think that all things can be explained by the interactions between atoms and molecules, and they are not sure that even atoms and molecules are totally lifeless and inert. Scientific materialism represents an older science, not the new science.

Still, there are many scientific materialists in our world. They are not necessarily scientists, but rather economists, politicians, and armchair philosophers for whom mechanistic ways of understanding offer a sense of control. Mechanistic worldviews generally picture the whole of reality in the analogy of a predictable and understandable machine—a computer, for example—the parts of which can be completely understood by human engineers. These worldviews are attractive because they give people a sense of mastery over the world, at the expense of feeling the Mystery that lies within it and beyond it.

Of course, people who imagine reality in the analogy of a vast and perfectly predictable machine know that feelings of Mystery exist. They know that people experience subjective states such as awe and wonder, love and forgiveness, fear and terror, hope and despair. But they will say that such states have no causal power in their own right. The "sense of Mystery" and "feelings of love" are products of real things, namely the atoms and molecules in the brain, but they lack causal power and cannot do anything on their own. They are like foam emerging from beer: the beer is the real thing; the foam is but a quasi-reality that lacks power and substance.

Materialists will then add, "If consciousness and feeling lack causal power in this way, then God and the Buddha-nature are even more vacuous. They are but mental abstractions produced by consciousness and feeling, which are themselves mere products of brain chemistry. They are illusions produced by the foam."

This book invites us to look at the world in a less mechanistic, more sacramental way. It invites us to imagine that the universe itself is evolving, that it is filled with something akin to consciousness or at least with energy that evolves into consciousness, and that we are in some way called, as human beings, to respond to the contemporary situation by helping create communities that are socially just, ecologically sustainable, and spiritually satisfying.

If you are Christian, I hope that you find something true in this way of seeing things. I trust that it is much closer to what you and I believe than is the worldview of the scientific materialist. We believe that the call comes from God, as mediated through the universe, the Earth, the Bible, our various traditions, and our own hopes. We believe that God is real and more than the heavens and the Earth, but we also believe that the heavens and the Earth are filled with God's beauty and God's Spirit. We have arrived at many worldviews over the centuries, but almost all of them want to speak of a living God in relation to a creative universe.

For the Christian, of course, having a good worldview is not the heart of Christianity. The heart of Christianity lies in practicing the presence of God in our daily lives, as individuals and as communities, in sound and silence, amid despair and hope. To practice this presence is to be available to God's Spirit both receptively and actively. It is to receive the presence of this Spirit as it flows through the shining of stars, the needs of the stranger, the rhythms of music, the laughter of friends, and the tears of the dying. And it is to respond to what is received with love and trust, gratitude and wonder, creativity and compassion. Kallistos Ware puts it clearly: "The whole aim of the Christian life is to be a Spirit-bearer, to live in the Spirit of God, to breathe the Spirit of God."[2]

Many Christians further recognize that even the materialist can breathe the Spirit. Even this materialist can be awed by a sunset and sensitive to the tears of the dying. He may think that those tears emanate from a brain that lacks a soul, but he is still moved by the emanations of that brain. "Having a good worldview" is not a necessary precondition for "practicing the presence." Right thinking is not necessary to right breathing.

Still, "having a good worldview" can help point individuals and communities in the right direction. This is especially the case if the worldview recognizes a spiritual dimension in life and includes some notion of God's Spirit. The worldview at issue may have different names for this Spirit. The Spirit may be called "the Tao" or "the Power that Connects" or "the Mystery of Life" or "the Sheer Wonder of Being" or "the Holy Spirit." The words are not so important. What is important is that the worldview point beyond itself to a world beyond words in which the Spirit is present.

The need for a good worldview is especially important in our age of consumerism. This is because there is an unhealthy worldview that is preached to us twenty-four hours a day on radio and television and that easily infects our lives unless we have a "good worldview" that can take its place. Its primary means of transmission is through mass media, and more particularly through advertisements on television.

The Worldview of Consumerism

This bad worldview is not atheism or materialism. It is the theology of consumerism. It can be found in people who think atheistically, presuming that matter-in-motion is what there is and all there is, but it can also be found in people who believe in God but who imagine God in a deistic way: that is, as a clockmaker who set everything in motion but who now watches from afar.

At the core of consumer theology is the view that this world of rocks and trees, hills and rivers is quite real and that it was "put here for us." Consumerism teaches us (1) that we are skin-encapsulated egos who are cut off from the world by the boundaries of our skin; (2) that the universe was created to meet our personal needs; (3) that the good life consists in consuming more and more each year; (4) that we are worthwhile as human beings if we are attractive, wealthy, and accomplished in the marketplace; and (5) that God, if God exists at all, is but a clockmaker who watches from afar, applauding our willful approach to life.

The Benefits of Consumerism

This worldview is not *all* bad. At least it has its defenders, who make plausible points. Admittedly, many of these defenders are corporate executives and financial officers who have vested interests in the theology of consumerism. They want people to subscribe to this theology because it increases their profits. But they do not apologize for these selfish motives. They argue that selfish motives are essential to human nature and that a theology of consumerism, with its inherent appeal to selfishness, offers the world three benefits.

First, it provides incentive for the creation of new goods and services, such as medicines, computers, and tractors, that lift people from drudgery and make people happier. The argument is that good things happen in our world, not particularly because people want to serve the common good but because they want to "get ahead," "beat out the competition," and "become successful." Their personal ambition leads them to invent and market goods that everybody enjoys. All people benefit from such ambition.

Second, consumerism gives people a sense of meaning and purpose in life, holding up the ideals of "upward mobility" and "success" as goals for human adventure. Human beings need to feel that they can grow and develop, that they can get ahead and reach the top. We are, as it were, genetically hardwired to be restless and exploratory, to want newness and novelty. Consumerism satisfies these needs by giving people "new things every year" and by providing them with a sense of the "top" toward which they can strive. This "top" is called success, and its three components are appearance, affluence, and marketable achievement.

Third, consumerism has the potential to unite people all over the world in a common consumer culture that, if given the chance, can offset the ancient hatreds and violence that are so often part of national and religious identities. The idea is that, as people learn to think of themselves as part of the "Pepsi Generation," they will be less inclined to think of themselves as "Christians" and "Muslims" and "Hindus" who kill each other in the name of deity, nation, and ethnic identity.

For the defenders of consumerism, these three benefits outweigh any costs. And indeed, there is truth in all of these arguments. The profit motive has resulted in goods that many people enjoy; the desire for material success does satisfy a need for adventure; and commitment to consumer values can replace ethnic hatred.

Nevertheless, there are opponents of consumerist theology. Implicitly, if not explicitly, they—we—assume that there are four costs to consumer theology, any one of which outweighs any alleged benefits. The empirical evidence for these costs is best presented elsewhere, but let me name them in broad strokes.

The Costs of Consumerism

First, the consumer mentality contributes to an overconsuming lifestyle that, as actively practiced by about one-fifth of the world's population, is unsustainable and unjust. It is unsustainable because it produces an enormous amount of pollution and waste, which has already resulted in problems such as global warming, and because it pulls more renewable resources from the Earth than the Earth can supply. It is unjust because it recommends a lifestyle that could not possibly be enjoyed by the other four-fifths of the world's population, given the limits to the Earth's resources and its capacities to absorb pollution.

Second, with its emphasis on the self as an isolated ego whose purpose is to "have my needs met," the consumer mentality contributes to a disregard for others and to a disintegration of family and community bonds. Overtly or covertly, it makes a virtue of greed and envy, thus adding to the world's violence, crime, family breakdown, and community disintegration. This is not an argument against free markets but rather an argument for moral sentiments—such as love, trust, and care for others—as essential underpinnings for any free market. When people live by market-driven values such as envy and ambition, and when they live by a worldview that elevates these values to ultimate values, things fall apart.

The third argument against consumerism concerns other forms of life. With its emphasis on the planet as mere resource for human use and on animals as mere commodities for human consumption, it leads to a disregard for the rights of wild animals to their habitats and the rights of domesticated animals (including those used for food) for freedom from suffering. When consumerism reigns, the planet itself becomes a collection of objects, not a communion of subjects. Biodiversity declines, and other living beings suffer.

The fourth argument concerns spirituality. With its emphasis on "being attractive, wealthy, and accomplished," consumerism neglects the deeper spiritual needs of human beings, which are to be wise, compassionate, and free. It taps into the human need for adventure but diverts this need toward trivial and destructive ends: "looking pretty," "being rich," and "being recognized by others." These ends do not satisfy the deeper yearnings of the human soul, which are to be linked with something larger and infinite: namely, God. In short, our souls are too big for consumerism, and consumerism is too small for our souls. Once we recognize this fact, we will need and want to undertake a deeper adventure, a more amazing journey. We will want to journey into God.

Alternatives to the Consumerist Worldview

In light of these costs, a very serious question emerges: Are there plausible and healthy alternatives to the theology of consumerism? More specifically, are there ways of understanding reality that make sense to us in light of what we know about the world; that speak to the human need for adventure; that respect the limits of the Earth and the rights of other creatures; and that help awaken us to our spiritual potential?

In answer to this question, there is good news and bad news. The good news is that there are many such worldviews, not just one. The bad news is that very few of them have the advertising skills of consumerism. These "minority perspectives" fall into four general groups:

- The worldviews of the world's religions, at least when those worldviews are freed from their incentives to violence and exclusivity. These include Christian theologies that emphasize God's love for the whole creation and the importance of following Christ in a life of simplicity. And they include Buddhist cosmologies that emphasize the interconnectedness of all things and the Buddha-nature within all creatures.
- The worldviews of modern science, when those worldviews are freed from mechanistic and reductionistic assumptions concerning the nature of matter. These include evolutionary worldviews, which stress a human kinship with the whole of creation and a continuum between consciousness and energy, and also quantum worldviews, which emphasize a creativity within the very depths of matter, such that evolution itself becomes a creative adventure in which humans participate.
- The worldviews of post-mechanistic philosophies, including those of ecofeminism and deep ecology, and those of individual philosophers—past and present—such as Alfred North Whitehead, Sri Aurobindo, Dogen, Thomas Berry.
- The worldviews of indigenous peoples from Asia, Africa, Latin America, and Oceania, whose ways of thinking are deeply ecological in orientation, showing how people can live responsibly and spiritually in local places.

I mention indigenous peoples at the end, not because they are less important, but because their worldviews have so often been unjustly appropriated by nonindigenous peoples. Nonindigenous peoples who learn from indigenous worldviews need to be mindful that a great deal has already been taken from indigenous peoples, particularly land, and that it is immoral to assume that "we" can "take" their worldviews too. At best, we can learn from their worldviews if, and only if, we are simultaneously involved in political action aimed at helping them survive.

The Hope for a Sustainable Future

Today there are many people from many walks of life who are interested in these post-mechanistic worldviews because they sense that, when combined with practical action and spiritual depth, these worldviews might contribute to a better world. Often these people do not know one another, and sometimes they feel quite isolated. They include homemakers and accountants, teachers and artists, nurses and plumbers, carpenters and physicians, young people and old people, Asians and Africans, Latin Americans and North Americans. One process theologian, John B. Cobb, Jr., calls them the Earthists.[3]

Of course, the word *Earthism* is an awkward and somewhat unappealing term. Cobb knows this. It is for lack of a better term that he uses the word *Earthist.* The people of whom he is speaking, and he counts himself among them, name themselves quite differently. Some speak of themselves as "evangelical Christians," some as "Orthodox Christians," some as "Roman Catholics," and some as "Quakers." Outside Christianity, some speak of themselves as "socially engaged Buddhists," some as "devout Muslims," and some as "radical feminists."

They have many differences, but amid their many differences, they have three things in common. The Earthists are (1) alienated from the theology of consumerism, (2) interested in a more spiritually sensitive way of living in the world, and (3) hopeful that they might contribute to a more sustainable world. By sustainability they often mean a combination of three things:

- Human well-being, including an elimination of abject poverty and ethnic violence
- Ecological integrity, including a respect for the habitats of wild animals and plants and compassion for animals under human domestication

- Economic viability, including a recovery of the value of small, community-based businesses that serve the community and are responsible to their customers

We process theologians consider ourselves among these people, and we call these people Earthists, not because we or they worship the Earth, but because they feel that the well-being of life on Earth is a better central organizing principle for modern societies than "economic growth for its own sake."

John Cobb further proposes that this spiritual movement—the Earthist movement—is an emerging movement within the larger sweep of Western history, which now exercises such an influence in many parts of the world. He suggests that in the West, three central organizing principles have heretofore held sway: Christianism, Nationalism, and Economism. Christianism was the central organizing principle in the Middle Ages. The energies and talents of many people in Western Europe were devoted to promoting the church as the center of public life. Nationalism replaced Christianism in the seventeenth century. The religious wars between Catholics and Protestants made it clear that "the church" was not the best organizing principle, because people would kill each other in the name of religion, and that "the nation" had more promise. In some circles, Economism began to replace Nationalism after World War II. The violence of two world wars and many smaller wars, which continues to this day, shows that "service to the nation" too often results in a desire to "destroy other nations" in the name of "national self-interest and national pride."

Economism puts forth "economic growth" as a more practical and serviceable goal for the human adventure. In our time, much of world history is a battle between Nationalism and Economism. Those who subscribe to Economism sometimes see Nationalism as a failed option, eventually to be superceded by a global market in which large corporations rule the world, with citizens becoming "consumers" who make choices among their options. The Nationalists resent this reduction of human life to consumerism and believe that a celebration of ethnic and religious identity is a better organizing principle.

Earthism, then, is an alternative both to Nationalism and Economism. The Earthist option suggests that service to life on Earth, with the help of the nation and the church and the corporation, is a better goal than any of the other three. This is not because such service will result in a utopia. There will always be problems. But it is because people do indeed live on a single planet, which they share with other creatures, and we can indeed devote our energies not to the idolatries of nation and religion and economy but to the well-being of others.

The Earthist movement, then, is a protest and an affirmation. It is a protest against Economism and its consumerist theology. And it is an affirmation of the possibility of a more just, sustainable, and spiritually satisfying world in which people live together in peace with one another, respectful of cultural traditions, and also in harmony with other animals and with the Earth.

In what follows, then, I introduce process theology as one among the many worldviews that might contribute to this Earthist hope and to a more spiritually satisfying way of living in the world.

Process Theology: The Key Ideas

Process theology is a form of Christian theology that emerged in the 1930s at the University of Chicago. It is influenced by the cosmological perspective of Alfred North Whitehead, and it has been adopted and developed by various Christian theologians, mostly Protestant but some Catholic. Whitehead's philosophy has also been used by Jews to develop a Jewish process theology and by Buddhists to develop a Buddhist process theology. Thus, it serves as a bridge for interreligious dialogue. Here are some of its key ideas.

The universe is an interconnected web of life. The first idea is that we humans are part of a larger web of life in which there are many different kinds of beings. This "web of life" is not limited to living beings on the planet Earth. It also includes atoms and molecules, hills and rivers, stars and galaxies; and it includes any other kinds of beings—spirits and ancestors, for example—that might exist in other planes of existence. All the beings are gathered together into a single network of interconnectedness, which the Bible calls "the Heavens and the Earth" and which we might also call "the universe."

All creatures in the universe have their own inner aliveness, and each living being has its own intrinsic value. The second idea is that the creatures in the universe—from atoms to animals—are "alive" in the sense that they have reality in and for themselves, even as they also have reality in and for others. And each living being, visible or invisible, has value in and for itself, even as it may have value for other living beings. A human being has intrinsic value, and so does a dog, an amoeba, an angel, a cancer cell, and an atom. The intrinsic value of a living being is its reality in and for itself.

There are gradations and kinds of intrinsic value relative to capacities for feeling and awareness. The third idea is that even as each living being has intrinsic value, there are different degrees and kinds of intrinsic value. For example, the kind and degree of intrinsic value that an atom has is itself different from the kind and degree of intrinsic value that a dog has. With the dog's greater capacity for feeling and awareness comes a special kind of intrinsic value that merits our moral respect. We need not worry about harming the atom, but we do indeed need to avoid harming the dog.

Each living being has instrumental value, positive or negative. The fourth idea is that each living being also has value for others, either positive or negative. A companion animal, for example, has positive instrumental value for the humans who love her, even as she also has value in and for herself. A cancer cell, on the other hand, has negative instrumental value for the body it inhabits, even as it has value in and for itself.

All creatures are immanent within one another, even as they transcend one another. The fifth idea is that each individual being in this web— each atom, for example—is influenced by every other being directly or indirectly, consciously or unconsciously. This might be called "the principle of interdependence" or "the principle of interconnectedness." Most of us understand this principle from the inside. We know that we ourselves are composed of the influences we receive from our bodies, our friends and family, the natural world, and a host of other factors. We are not islands unto ourselves. Process theology proposes that this is true of all beings. Each entity in the universe—each atom, each molecule, each spirit, each ancestor—is partly composed of the influences it receives from its immediate surroundings and its wider environment. No creature is an island.

The universe is inherently creative. The sixth idea is that even as each being is influenced by all other beings, each being also contains within itself a spark of creativity, on the basis of which it responds to those influences. Again, most of us know this from personal experience. We know that even as we are influenced by myriad factors in our environment and our personal past, we have some degree of freedom, in the present moment, for responding to those influences.

For process theologians, this freedom is an expression of, not an exception to, what is found throughout nature. It is what lies behind the "principle of uncertainty" or the "principle of indeterminacy" in quantum physics. This principle states that even if we know with certainty all the conditions that will influence an emerging submicroscopic event, the behavior of that event is not predictable, because the event is not entirely determined by those conditions. In addition to these influences, the emerging event contains within itself a capacity to actualize one among several possibilities for responding to, and thus integrating, those influences.

In process theology, this actualization of a possibility—be it on the part of an atom or a living cell or human being—is what is meant by "creativity." Understood in this sense, creativity is not necessarily conscious or intentional. The "creativity" of a living cell, for example, probably does not involve conscious intention. Nor is this creativity necessarily good. If the living cell happens to be a cancer cell, for example, then that cell is "creative" in the possibilities it actualizes for growth within a human body, but its creativity is destructive rather than constructive for the body as a whole. There is much creativity in our universe that is destructive rather than constructive.

To speak of a "creative" universe is to suggest that all beings in the universe are partly free and partly determined. Of course, many beings—atoms and cancer cells, for example—are almost completely determined, and their creativity is quite miniscule. They may well be 99.9 percent determined and less than 1 percent free. Other beings—humans, for example—may contain larger degrees of creativity. In any case, no being is completely determined by its environmental influences.

The universe is constantly evolving. The seventh idea is that, by virtue of the creativity just noted, the universe as a whole cannot and ought not to be described as a "mere machine" with a predetermined or precisely determined end. The universe does not run like a clock. It is better described as an ongoing creative process in which new events are being added at each moment; in which each creature plays a part, no matter how small; and in which habits emerge, over long stretches of time, that become "laws of nature" for the creatures at issue.

One analogy to this creative process might be the music of a symphony orchestra. Each being in the universe would be a member of the orchestra, and the music produced by this orchestra—the music of the spheres—would be the ongoing and yet unfinished "symphony" that is being produced by these members. The symphony would be harmonious in some respects, disharmonious in others, and ever changing. From the vantage point of process theology, the symphony has no preordained end that is determined in advance by an already existing score. There is a very general score, which determines the general rules under which nature unfolds, but the specifics are determined by the players themselves.

Another name for this creative process is "evolution." From the vantage point of process theologians, evolution is an exploratory process on the part of the universe, and it has occurred and is still occurring at many levels: galactic, geological, biological, cultural, and spiritual. In no instance is evolution a strictly mechanistic process. It is always a "continuing creation" in which the myriad beings of "the heavens and Earth" actualize new possibilities.

The universe unfolds moment by moment. The eighth idea is that the life histories of the orchestral players—the atoms, the living cells, the human beings—are divisible into moments of experience.

This idea contradicts a modern, Western view that tends to view "essences" of things in solid and substantial terms. Sometimes we think of the "essence" or "soul" of a human being, for example, in the analogy of a solid and substantial entity, such as a rock, that endures unchanged over time. We say that the "soul" with which we are born is precisely the "soul" with which we die.

From the vantage point of process theology, this view is incorrect. The soul is actually a series of experiential moments, each of which inherits both consciously and unconsciously from predecessor experiences, and each of which contributes, for good or ill, to successor experiences. There is no solid and substantial entity underlying this succession of experiences; we ourselves are the succession of experiences, moment by moment.

Moreover, we do not stand outside this succession watching it from afar. It is not as if the succession of experiences is a river flowing by us, and we are standing outside this river watching it from a third-person perspective. Rather, we are in the river, swimming. Each stroke of our arms is a "present moment of experience," and at each instance we ourselves are the stroking.

Process theologians further add that atoms and living cells are also composed of such "present moments." If we imagine ourselves inside a living cell, for example, we realize that the cell, too, consists of moment-by-moment responses to its immediate cellular environment. These moment-by-moment responses are its own "experience," albeit unconscious rather than conscious.

The same applies to an atom. An atom consists of momentary "quantum events" or "energy events," which arise and perish in a momentary way, each inheriting from predecessors and each contributing to successors. A "quantum event" within the depths of an atom is a submicroscopic analog to a "moment of experience" in a human lifetime. The momentary experiences composing a human life are a highly evolved expression of the energy events composing an electron. The history of the universe is itself an evolution from energy into consciousness, with both energy and consciousness occurring moment by moment.

God is the Subjective Unity of the universe. The ninth idea is that this creative and moment-by-moment universe unfolds within the larger context of an infinite Clearing—an Open Space—that is everywhere at once. This infinite Clearing is the Mystery at the heart of the universe, and it is presupposed every time we speak of the "ultimate unity" of the universe. This unity is that to which Muslims point when they say "Allah," to which Christians point when they say "God," to which Jews point when they say "Adonai," and to which Hindus point when they say "Brahman." It is not outside the universe in a separate plane of existence; it is that within which we ourselves, and all other beings in any plane of existence, live and breathe and have our being.

God is more than all things added together. The tenth idea is that this Open Space is not an empty vacuum that adds nothing to the universe, but rather a sky-like Mind filled with Wisdom, Compassion, and Freedom. The universe itself participates in this Wisdom, Compassion, and Freedom; but the Wisdom, Compassion, and Freedom are also more than the universe itself. This is what it means to say that God "transcends" the universe. It does not mean that God is located in another region of space. Rather, it means that there is always more to Wisdom, Compassion, and Freedom—and thus more to God—than our experience comprehends. The transcendence of God is this more-ness.

For process theologians, this insight emerges from the wisdom of the many world religions. It is what Christians, Jews, Muslims, and Hindus "know" from their own religious experiences. They know that they receive wisdom, compassion, and freedom from a deeper source; and they know that there is always more to Wisdom, Compassion, and Freedom than their experiences comprehend. This spiritual knowing is complementary to the insights of modern science. To say that God "enriches" the universe is to say that the universe is at home in the larger context of a Hospitable Habitat: a Wisdom, Compassion, and Freedom that transcends us but that includes us.

God feels the feelings of all creatures, sharing in their sufferings and joys. The eleventh idea is that this sky-like Mind shares in the joys and sufferings of each creature, on its own terms and for its own sake. For process theologians, this idea can be found in many religions, but it is especially important in the teachings of Jesus, who teaches that the Mystery at the heart of the universe—God—loves even the smallest of sparrows, on its own terms and for its own sake.

God breathes within each creature. The twelfth idea is that this Mind is within each creature, at each and every moment of its life, beckoning that creature toward the fullness of life, relative to what is possible for it in the situation at hand. It is by virtue of this indwelling presence that new forms of order have emerged over time within evolution and that we discern a general tendency toward consciousness and complexity despite the countervailing effects of entropy.

Even the stars pray. The thirteenth idea is that all things in the universe experience the luring presence of God at a prereflective and preconscious level and that they respond to this presence in one way or another. Their response is their prayer, their way of addressing God. In the case of human beings, we respond consciously and unconsciously, because much of our own experience is unconscious rather than conscious. Even if we are not aware of the inner beckoning of the Mind at a conscious level, it is within us, at a very deep level, as our own inner teacher. If we respond to this inner teacher, even if unintentionally and unconsciously, we become more whole as human beings.

There are three fruits of full humanity—the three ways in which we respond to the deep calling of God: wisdom, compassion, and freedom. The freedom is a freedom from greed, hatred, and resentment; it is a freedom for being present to others and ourselves in wise and compassionate ways. We are made in the image of God, so the Bible tells us, and our task is to grow into God's likeness.

God's prayer is for holy communion. The fourteenth idea is that God's prayer within human life—the call toward wisdom, compassion, and freedom—is a call toward holy communion. It is a call to enter into rich relationships with the surrounding world, human and nonhuman, and to help create communities in which such communion is affirmed and nurtured. This means that the call of God within human life is not simply toward individual well-being, important as that is, but also toward work and struggle to create what Martin Luther King, Jr., calls "beloved communities."

This call to create beloved communities involves four guidelines, which are enunciated in a document called the "Earth Charter."[4] This character reveals the deepest impulses of the Earthist hope. We are beckoned by God to

- Respect Earth and life in all its diversity

- Care for the community of life with understanding, compassion, and love
- Build democratic societies that are just, participatory, sustainable, and peaceful
- Secure Earth's bounty and beauty for present and future generations

From the perspective of process theology, these four guidelines for action are part of the "great work" of human life. The Great Work is not only to be whole as individuals and amid personal relationships, it is also to be in the process of creating communities that express the will of God "on Earth as it is in heaven."

Change is needed. The fifteenth idea is that the building of beloved communities involves a critique of consumerism, leading to a simplification of lifestyles among the overconsumers of the world, and a transformation of the political and economic spheres of life, which would include a transformation of the professions—medicine, law, education, business, and religion—so that they serve the interests of the community of life on earth. The Great Work thus involves people's utilizing their gifts within these professions to change the professions, committing themselves to Earthist rather than Economistic ideals. The central organizing principle thus needs to become respect for the community of life rather than economic growth for its own sake.

Humility is needed. The sixteenth idea is that the very struggle to build beloved and sustainable communities, and the firm-but-gentle holding of convictions conducive to that end (as exemplified in the previous fifteen ideas), requires humility before the fact that our understanding of God's will for the Earth and God's will itself are not necessarily identical. The Spirit can work in the lives of plants, animals, and people quite independently of our efforts, and its directions can surprise us. The struggle to build beloved communities is best understood as an act of cooperating with the Spirit, not manipulating it, cognizant that God's Breathing is always more than our ideas and experiences of it.

Spirituality is needed. The seventeenth idea is that this humility is part of the very purpose of life, which is to live from the Center, without claiming to have mastered the Center from which we live. More specifically, the humility is part of the wisdom of living from the Center, which, when combined with compassion and freedom, is the heart of life. The point here is that efforts to change the world, particularly when guided by religious rhetoric, need to be grounded in a deeper spirituality, aware of the world beyond words, or they easily become idolatrous.

Spirituality is eternal life. The eighteenth idea is that living from the Center is itself a participation in the deeper life—the Eternal Life—that is the sky-like Mind itself. Understood in this sense, eternal life is not necessarily a continuation of the soul's existence after death, although it may involve such continuation until wholeness is realized. Recall the previous chapter, in which I suggested that small boys falling from tall buildings—Eric Morris, to be specific—can indeed enjoy spiritual growth after death, in other planes of existence. For me and for other process theologians, this hope for growth after death is plausible precisely because there are other planes of existence (the universe is a multiverse) and the soul is not exactly identical with its body. From the perspective of process theology, it is possible that all living beings enjoy life after death until they grow into that fullness, that likeness of God, to which they are called, each in its own way.

Still, in speaking of eternal life at the end of this book, I do not mean the continued existence of the psyche after death. Rather, I mean a participation in the very life of the Divine, here and now, even if there is no life after death. The purpose of this book has been to point toward this kind of eternal life. It can last but a moment, and yet it participates in a deeper eternity that is beyond all moments.

Eternal life is communal. The nineteenth idea is that our participation in eternity invites and requires attention to the deep connectedness of all living beings, such that we realize that, in our moments of full aliveness, the situations of others are included in our own aliveness. Their suffering is our suffering; their joy is our joy. There is no private nirvana, no private heaven. There is only the fact that we become fully alive, fully awakened, as nodes in a larger web of life, itself enfolded in a deeper love. This means that we are never quite saved alone, that salvation needs others to be complete. Insofar as others still suffer, the quality of our own eternal life is not yet complete. We truly know eternity not when we say "Now I know eternal life" but rather when we pray "May all beings be happy" and then help them find the happiness they seek. Eternal life is love.

Let it go. The twentieth and final idea, also espoused by process theology, is that process theology is not itself absolute. This means that all the ideas named above are but fleeting attempts to verbalize intuitions that are deeper than words, and that even if the intuitions are true, they ought not to be clung to as if they were the final story. Practically speaking, this means that you, the reader, might wish to affirm some of them but not all of them.

For my part, I suspect that ideas dealing with God's Breathing are the most important. I know many people who live from this Breathing in their lives, but who look at the world quite differently than I do. Some are more liberal than I, and some more conservative. Some belong to other religions, and some to no religion. I suspect that the God who breathes is much more interested in the fact that they live from the Breathing than that they agree with me, or I with them, about the Breathing from which they live. Process theology is helpful because it offers a clear and plausible alternative to the consumerist worldview, but it becomes idolatrous in its own right if it even hints at mastery of the deeper Breathing from which life emerges. What is most important is that we live from the Breathing, each in our own way. In this living there is a wisdom deeper than words and worldviews. It is eternal life, moment by moment.

Conclusion

All That Really Matters

...god is a transparency that drenches everything you help us notice...You sweet theologian: you grew new names for god: gourmet, cleaning woman, jazz, spring snow.
> Coleman Barks,[1] a poet from Georgia, writing of
> another poet, Bill Matthews, who died in 1997

Wisdom is more than words. It may enter our lives through music, art, feelings, dreams, silence, and the palpable presence of the universe itself. In the first chapter I introduced a young student who received wisdom through the quiet listening of good friends. In the second chapter I presented a stroller who received wisdom through the enormous and complicated eyes of a grasshopper. In the fifth chapter I introduced a woman who received wisdom through the encompassing presence of a dark and starlit sky. In each instance they received revelation in nonverbal ways. Through intuition and felt presence, not abstract concepts, they discovered the truth of holy communion.

Nevertheless, our lives can also be enriched by worldviews that help us appreciate what we learn in nonverbal ways. Such worldviews can help us know that the universe itself is a communion of subjects, not a collection of objects, and that we can add to this communion. We can add to the communion by listening to others in quiet, nonjudgmental ways, by gazing into the eyes of grasshoppers and appreciating their wild and precious lives, and by helping create communities that are free from greed and free for love. This is the Great Work of our lives. It may be hidden to others, but it is visible to the deeper Communion. It is visible to God.

159

In chapter 6 I recommended process theology as a worldview that might help us appreciate nonverbal intuitions. This theology affirms that there are many ways of knowing: musical, bodily, shamanic, domestic, poetic, mathematical, scientific, emotional, and theological. I hope that, in some small way, this book has helped you and me alike to recognize our own capacities for some of these ways. Perhaps it has helped us become better dreamers, better listeners, better homemakers, better laughers, better sleepers. Even better theologians.

If it has helped us become better theologians, let it be for the right reasons. Let it *not* be because we are more attached to the word *God.* Sometimes it helps to write God with a little *g* rather than an uppercase *G,* in order to free us from too much word-clinging. Too much wordolatry. Too much fundamentalism. God is always more than our concepts of God. And our names too.

Let it be because we are better able to find the God who is more than words: the God who is found in the very presence of healthy food, the cleaning woman, jazz, and spring snow. And who is found in the presence of a mysterious and womblike Love who hears us when we say "Dear God, I want you," "Dear God, I need you," "Dear God, I am so sorry," or "Dear God, it is all so beautiful."

In this book I have wanted to affirm this very God: the encircling Presence who hears prayers and who is found in jazz and the cleaning woman. I have spoken of the presence of this God as God's Breathing. I have suggested that, if we listen to this Breathing in a deep way, we will want to get down on our knees next to the cleaning woman and scrub the floors. We might also want to help her stand up, stretch, and go home. This, too, is the Great Work. It is bodily and domestic and ordinary and holy. It is not puffed up. It does not ride in limousines. It sees past the illusions of appearance, affluence, and marketable achievement. It lives from the Center.

To live from the Center: this is what it comes to. It is the Way of Jesus and the Buddha. Of Mother Teresa and the Dalai Lama. Of the cleaning woman and the jazz musician. Of the lilies and the grasshoppers. It is eternal life, moment by moment. It is all that really matters. Even the stars pray.

Notes

Prologue

[1]Emily Dickinson, as quoted by Kathleen Norris in *The Cloister Walk* (New York: Riverhead Books, 1996), 222.

[2]Mary Daly, *Gyn/Ecology: The Metaethics of Radical Feminism* (Boston: Beacon Press, 1990), 466.

Introduction

[1]Naomi Shihab Nye, "Welcome," in *Prayers for a Thousand Years*, ed. Elizabeth Roberts and Elias Amidon (San Francisco: Harper San Francisco, 1999), 123.

[2]Brother Lawrence, *The Practice of the Presence of God* (Springdale, Pa.: Whitaker House, 1982).

[3]Alan Durning, *How Much Is Enough? Consumer Society and the Fate of the Earth* (New York: Norton, 1992), 37–48.

[4]Ibid., 49–61.

[5]Ibid., 149.

[6]Frederick Buechner, *Wishful Thinking: A Theological ABC* (New York: Harper & Row, 1973).

[7]Thomas Berry, *The Great Work: Our Way into the Future* (New York: Bell Tower, 1999), 16.

[8]See Jay McDaniel, *With Roots and Wings* (Maryknoll, N.Y.: Orbis Books, 1995).

[9]Herman Daly and John Cobb, Jr., *For the Common Good: Redirecting the Economy toward Community, the Environment, and a Sustainable Future* (Boston: Beacon Press, 1994).

[10]Ibid., 138.

[11]See Thomas Merton, *Contemplative Prayer* (New York: Herder and Herder, 1969), and *Mystics and Zen Masters* (New York: Farrar, Strauss, and Giroux, 1967).

Chapter One

[1]Bishop Kallistos Ware, *The Orthodox Way* (New York: St. Vladimir's Seminary Press, 1995), 90.

[2]See Thomas Kelly, *A Testament of Devotion* (San Francisco: Harper San Francisco, 1992), 5.

[3]Ibid., 92

[4]George Soros, as quoted in *Atlantic Monthly* 281, no. 1: 24.

[5]C. S. Lewis, *Mere Christianity* (New York: Walker and Co., 1999), 65.

[6]Ibid., 65.

[7]See Pattiann Rogers, "The Greatest Grandeur," in *Firekeeper: New and Selected Poems* (Minneapolis: Milkweed Editions, 1994), 205.

[8]Ibid.

[9]Ibid.

Chapter Two

[1]Thich Nhat Hanh, *Living Buddha, Living Christ* (New York: Riverhead Books, 1995), 23.

[2]Mary Oliver, "The Summer Day," in *House of Light* (Boston: Beacon Press, 1990), 60.

[3]Ibid.

[4]Huston Smith, quotation taken from "The Wisdom of Faith with Huston Smith: A Bill Moyers Special," Public Broadcasting System, 1996.

[5]Durning, *How Much Is Enough?*

[6]Ibid., 26.

[7]See William Leach, *Land of Desire: Merchants, Power, and the Rise of a New American Culture* (New York: Vintage Books, 1993).

[8]Ibid., 18.

[9]Lawrence Ferlinghetti, "Christ Climbed Down," in *A Coney Island of the Mind* (New York: New Directions, 1958), 69–70.

[10]The phrase appears in Gerard Manley Hopkins' "God's Grandeur," as found in *The Norton Anthology of Modern Poetry*, ed. Richard Ellmann and Robert O' Clair (New York: Norton, 1988), 101.

Chapter Three

[1]Gerald Stern, "Lucky Life," in *Lucky Life* (Boston: Houghton Mifflin, 1977), 43.

[2]Hopkins, "God's Grandeur."

[3]"Metta Sutra," quoted in *Entering the Stream: An Introduction to the Buddha and his Teachings* (Boston: Shambhala, 1993), 142.

[4]See *The Oxford English Dictionary,* 2nd ed., vol. 7 (Oxford: Clarendon Press, 1989), 1097.

[5]See Michael Argyle, *The Psychology of Happiness* (New York: Methuen, 1987).

[6]Victor Frankl, *Man's Search for Meaning* (Boston: Beacon Press, 1963).

[7]Howard Thurman, *Jesus and the Disinherited* (Boston: Beacon Press, 1996), 50.

[8]This was first written when Mother Teresa was still alive, and I have left it unchanged.

[9]"Metta Sutra," *Entering the Stream,* 142.

Chapter Four

[1]Ibn Al-Arabi, quoted in Huston Smith, *The World's Religions* (San Francisco: Harper San Francisco, 1991), 264.

[2]This image is taken from Phillip Booth's poem "First Lesson," in *Strong Measures: Contemporary American Poetry in Traditional Forms,* ed. Philip Dacey and David Jauss (New York: HarperCollins, 1986).

[3]St. John of the Cross, *The Dark Night of the Soul* (Cambridge, U.K.: James Clarke and Co., 1973).

[4]See Don Richard Riso, *Personality Types: Using the Enneagram for Self-Discovery* (Boston: Houghton Mifflin, 1990).

[5]See St. John of the Cross, *The Dark Night of the Soul.*

[6]See Judson Jerome, "Eve: Night Thoughts," in *Strong Measures: Contemporary American Poetry in Traditional Forms*, ed. Philip Dacey and David Jauss (New York: HarperCollins, 1986), 153.

[7]Richard Foster, *Prayer: Finding the Heart's True Home* (San Francisco: Harper San Francisco, 1992), 155.

[8]Ware, *The Orthodox Way,* 105–6.

[9]Ibid.

[10]Ibid., 119.

[11]For a good introduction to Zen meditation and its place in the life of a practicing Christian, see Ruben L. F. Habito, *Healing Breath: Zen Spirituality for a Wounded Earth* (Maryknoll, N. Y.: Orbis Books, 1996), 38–57.

Chapter Five

[1]Pattiann Rogers, "Distance and Depth," in *Firekeeper* (Minneapolis: Milkweed Editions, 1994), 189–90.

[2]Julian of Norwich, *Showings,* trans. Edmund College and James Walsh (New York: Paulist Press, 1978), 225.

[3]Roy Scheele, "A Gap in the Cedar," in *Strong Measures: Contemporary American Poetry in Traditional Forms*, ed. Philip Dacey and David Jauss (New York: HarperCollins, 1986), 70.

[4]As cited by Ware, *The Orthodox Way,* 43.

[5]Ibid., 43–44.

[6]Rogers, "Distance and Depth," in *Firekeeper.*

[7]Julian of Norwich, *Showings.*

Chapter Six

[1]See Alfred North Whitehead, *Science in the Modern World* (New York: Free Press, 1967).
[2]Ware, *The Orthodox Way,* 90.
[3]John B. Cobb, Jr., *The Earthist Challenge to Economism: A Theological Critique of the World* (New York: St. Martin's Press, 1999), 35–41.

[4]"The Earth Charter is a statement of fundamental ethical principles and practical guidelines of enduring significance that are widely shared by all people. In like manner to the U.N. Declaration on Human Rights, it will serve as a universal code of conduct to guide people and nations towards sustainable development. It is a call for action that has an integrated vision and adds significant new dimensions to what has been expressed in earlier agreements and declarations on the environment and sustainable development. The Earth Charter is also a process—a People's movement. It is a participatory process that engages individuals and groups in dialogues on shared values and encourages all to embody the Earth Charter principles in our lifestyles and decisions." (Taken from the Earth Charter Web page, http://www.earthcharter.org/, where the entire Earth Charter can be read in many different languages.)

Conclusion

[1]Coleman Barks, "Bill Matthews Coming Along (1942–1997)," in *The Best American Poetry*, ed. David Lehman and Robert Bly (New York: Scribner Paperback Poetry, 1999), 37.

Index